HOW

WE

PREVENT

WEALTH

Romeo Jeremiah Clayton

PRINTED IN THE UNITED STATES OF AMERICA

This book is designed to provide accurate and authoritative information
on the subject of personal finances. It is sold with the understanding
that neither the Author nor the Publisher is engaged in rendering legal,
accounting, or other professional services by publishing this book. As
each individual situation is unique, questions relevant to personal
finances and specific to the individual should be addressed to an
appropriate professional to ensure that the situation has been evaluated
carefully and appropriately. The Author and Publisher specifically
disclaim any liability, loss, or risk which is incurred as a consequence,
directly or indirectly, of the use and application of any of the contents
of this work.

First edition. Published May 2011

Cover Design by: Enrique Chumbes Lozano

ISBN-13:
978-1461004592

ISBN-10:
1461004594

For my son,

Romeo Jr.

In hopes that he does not become a

"wealth preventer."

A special acknowledgement to,

Anree Little,

Rebecca Clayton,

James Drumgole,

Mike Bocchino,

Lamar Ager,

Dan Gackowski,

Sean Helmbrecht,

Sandra Norwood, and

Diane Caine.

Thank you for either being a dedicated follower of my writings, for actually listening to my countless reflections about money, or for giving me your encouragement and inspiration to write this book.

Contents

Preface

These were my approximate adjusted gross earnings for the last 13 years:

- Year 1: $7,900
- Year 2: $7,500
- Year 3: $18,000
- Year 4: $28,800
- Year 5: $11,500
- Year 6: $20,000
- Year 7: $34,500
- Year 8: $50,000
- Year 9: $40,000
- Year 10: $48,000
- Year 11: $51,000
- Year 12: $ 57,000
- Year 13: $68,000

For a total of: $442,200.

Yet, my total savings in Year 13 was only $45,000; about $40,000 in retirement savings and $5,000 in my child's college savings.

Some may argue that $45,000 is plenty saved for someone who is thirty years old, but the problem is that I could have absolutely saved more given my relatively high, but short lifetime earnings thus far. When I think about all my past, unwise financial decisions, $45,000 is just pittance compared to what I *could have* saved to this point; there is no reason why I couldn't have easily saved $100,000 or more.

Knowing this information, I started asking the question, "Why don't I have at least $100,000 saved?" Then I started reflecting. I realized I had purchased plenty of cars that I no longer have, paid plenty in credit card interest, purchased a home that I am still paying a mortgage for but not living in, and have even purchased shares of stocks that I no longer own and had sold at a lost. Additionally, as my income grew, so did my standard of living.

It was shortly before I turned thirty-years-old when I realized that I'd prevented myself from amassing wealth. It wasn't my job, the government, or a white collar crime. It was my own financial decisions that redirected my income to other areas other than savings.

How We Prevent Wealth is mainly based on my personal financial mistakes made in the past and those that I am currently trying to correct. I started realizing how I, along with many others prevent ourselves from building wealth. Hence, I came up with the name for this book. This book serves as an outlet for me to share my mistakes, and for others who are doing similar things to reflect on them and do better so that they may have greater financial success.

I am not a personal financial planner or a professional writer, and I hold no professional certifications dealing in finance. I have earned my MBA, but *an MBA is no certification in personal finance*. My credentials, so to speak, are based mainly in accomplishments, not academics. My biggest financial accomplishment was the realization that we are our own worst enemy, and it has taken me thirty years to figure this out. By leveraging off of this "new found" knowledge, I hope to now successfully build and accumulate wealth far greater than I have in the past.

Why should you read this book? Because you can most likely relate to all of the presented scenarios, reflect on them, and subsequently choose to make wiser financial decisions for yourself. I have come to the conclusion that it's not how little we earn; it's the accumulation of unwise decisions that prevents us from building wealth.

How We Prevent Wealth

Introduction

There are no magic formulas for building wealth in the world of personal finance. If you have been following personal finance for a while, there are usually "no new lessons learned" among books, radio shows, leaflets, Web sites, television shows, or any financial sources when it comes to making smart personal financial decisions. They are all variations of the following:

- Spend less than you earn
- Minimize interest paid
- Save money for your future

Yet, somehow there continues to be a *wealth gap* between the rich and the poor in many of the richest, most developed, and most prosperous nations; many of us wonder why. Ultimately the explanations lie within us; we are our own "financial enemies." It has taken me a relatively long time to figure this out, but I'm glad that I finally did.

Chances are if you are reading this book, you already have a working knowledge about the ideas involved in managing personal finances. You most likely know what a budget is and what it means to "live within your means." You probably are aware of different investment tools for retirement, the effect of poor credit scores, and other aspects of personal finance. So, while this book delves into some of these ideas, it is by no means a book with the sole purpose of teaching these basics, but rather a calling of self-awareness to take the knowledge you may already have, or at least have heard at some time or another, and actually apply it.

This book is intended to reflect on the things that we may do wrong, and to highlight the obstacles we place in our own way that prevent us from closing this wealth gap. Hopefully in the end, we'll correct our mistakes and eventually do things better—or at least we'll be more conscious of our financial activities. Thus, we should be able to accumulate, rather than prevent our wealth.

Chapter 1

I Prevent Wealth

Turning thirty years old was a significant milestone for me. It represented much more than just getting older.

The driving force for this book was a realization of where I stood financially at almost thirty years old, compared to where I should have been. On my birthday, a particular reality of my life dawned on me—I'd been in the work force for over twelve years.

I started thinking about all of the ill-informed and impulsive financial decisions that I'd made over the last twelve years. I remember bringing home a salary of approximately $20,000 annually as a newly enlisted member in the Navy, and I've since grown to earn almost four times that amount. In those years, I'd bought at least nine different cars, stopped and started a retirement account five different times, invested in mutual funds and pulled out the market at a loss, invested in stocks and pulled out the market at a loss; and purchased a number of large-screen televisions, multiple sets of furniture, various memberships to wholesale clubs, and many other things.

Of course, not all of my money went to frivolous spending—but I can't really think of any smart expenditure as of this moment, other than paying off student loans and debt that I had accumulated. To be a bit self-critical, paying off these loans was not too big of an accomplishment for me, because I've always hated—and will always hate—debt. Getting rid of it was more of an inborn obsession than an intentional move to improve my finances. I have always been smart not to purchase things with credit cards more than necessary, but when I did, paying the least amount of interest that I could was a top priority for me. If I took out a loan, I would always pay it off before the term expired. But despite these good financial moves, after thinking for only a short time, I came to the conclusion that *it was me and only me who had prevented me from being where I should be financially.*

I started thinking, what *if* my spouse and I had kept our first cars and not purchased the following eight cars? What *if* I had continued to put the maximum amount of money into my IRA and kept it there from age nineteen? What *if* I had kept my money in the stocks that I had purchased when I was nineteen, twenty-three, or twenty-seven years old? Or what *if* I had continued to rent where I was living instead of purchasing a home when I knew I would be moving in less than three years because of my military career? I continued to ask myself, what *if*?

How We Prevent Wealth

Well, the answers to the questions no longer matter. The question is now: *What am I going to do better?* Like time, the money that I've made poor decisions with cannot be taken back. It's pretty clear that I've stopped myself from accumulating more than my family should have in savings. My situation is not uncommon, however. In fact, many who are turning thirty years old this year, or any age, are facing tougher financial situations than ever before; jobs are scarce and unstable, and world economies are heavily in debt. It is not as easy for everyone to recover from their mistakes once they dig themselves into giant financial holes. *So, what should we do about it*? Is the answer as simple as not making the same mistakes over? How would we know what our mistakes are?

Hence, *How We Prevent Wealth.* This book is a journey to realizing how we prevent ourselves from accumulating wealth. Having begun this journey myself, I make myself accountable to the world. I will share with whoever will listen, the mistakes that I've made even while intuitively always knowing the right answers. I encourage everyone to take the time and think about what it is they do to prevent themselves from obtaining wealth. My realization has already been made: now it is time for me to start over and do something about it.

I Prevent Wealth

Chapter 2

We Don't Believe Wealth Is Within Our Reach

What Is Wealth?

Does being wealthy necessarily mean being rich? If not, how would you then define wealth?

For the sake of this text, I'm going to define wealth as having financial freedom. Financial freedom is the ability to go on a vacation, play with our grandchildren, read a book, learn a language, golf when the weather is beautiful, fish when the bass are most active, or play a video game all day without having to worry about money. Financial freedom is about living the last third of our lives without worrying about going to a job. It is an actual retirement.

I argue that there should be no one working past sixty years of age if they don't have the desire to do so. Yet, more and more, we see people working in their "golden years," not because they want to, but because they have to. I submit that the "golden years" should truly be golden, and depending on our current age and how aggressively we prepare, our golden years can possibly start at a much younger age than sixty. So, now the question becomes, how do *we* prevent ourselves from having financial freedom?

We prevent our wealth or financial freedom with the choices that we make. We *choose* to pay the banks rather than ourselves first. We *choose* to not further educate ourselves, formally or informally, so that we can earn more over our lifetime. We *choose* our own demise.

Wealth is not about having plenty of money now, per se; one can have plenty of money but still have many financial obligations. Wealth is about accumulating enough money over a working lifetime that we are eventually able to live a life free from financial worries. There would be no need to worry as to whether the mortgage, our children's college tuition, or any other payments will be made if we are living wealthy; those obligations would either be already paid or could be paid for with money that we have on-hand. Wealth is possible for many of us if we make smart financial decisions. Yet, there are so many of us who *choose* not to have their wealth materialize.

What Is Your Net Worth Now?

A quick way to assess how wealthy we are is to determine our net worth. In a sense, net worth means little; it's not necessarily a number that we can quickly turn into cash. But it *is* a way to determine how well off we'd be if we were to lose our job and sell off all of our assets.

The net worth formula is quite simple. We have to add up all of our assets (I like to use things that we can readily sell) and then subtract all of our debt liabilities. For the sake of this equation, and to make our lives simpler, our assets should include big items only, such as cars, homes, retirement accounts, savings accounts, checking accounts, cash on hand, and funds in any brokerage accounts (such as college funds, stocks, or bonds). Liabilities should include anything that you owe money on, such as loans, credit cards, rental properties, time shares, or mortgages. These things are what we should strive to minimize. Once we determine the total number for both, we simply subtract the liabilities from the assets to determine our net worth.

Use the figure on the next page to determine your current net worth.

We Don't Believe Wealth Is Within Our Reach

Assets		Liabilities	
IRA/TSP/401(k)s	$_____	Signature Loans	$_____
Cash on hand	$_____	Auto Loans	$_____
Checking Accounts	$_____	Consolidation Loans	$_____
Savings Accounts	$_____	Student Loans	$_____
Money Market/ Bonds/CDs	$_____	Credit Cards (Total Balance on all)	$_____
Mutual Funds	$_____	Real Estate Mortgage Balances	$_____
Brokerage Accounts	$_____	Other Liabilities	$_____
Vehicles	$_____		
Real Estate (Market Values)	$_____		
Other Assets	$_____		
Total Assets	$_____	Total Liabilities	$_____
		Net Worth (Assets- Liabilities)	$_____

Determine Your Net Worth

What Should Your Net Worth Be?

According to Thomas J. Stanley and William D. Danko, the authors of "The Millionaire Next Door," a thirty-year-old individual whose annual income is $50,000 should have accumulated $150,000 in net worth. To determine this figure you would simply, "multiply your age times your realized pretax annual household income from all sources except inheritances" and then "divide by ten." Hence, ($50,000 x 30)/10 = $150,000. Given this formula, a fifty-year-old individual with $50,000 in annual income should have a net worth of at least $250,000. Of course, this is only a "rule of thumb," but it doesn't hurt to use it as a guideline.

If we first look at the case of the thirty-year-old who makes $50,000 a year pretax, one may argue that there are many valid reasons why his or her net worth should deviate far from $150,000. One of many valid reasons is that the worker may have recently graduated college, just started a career, or recently started a family. Anyone who has started a family knows that there are associated start-up costs such as a wedding, purchasing things for a new home, or having children. If one graduates with student loans, there are even more valid reasons why $150,000 will be far off.

We Don't Believe Wealth Is Within Our Reach

Although there can be many valid excuses for the thirty-year-old worker, there should not be many excuses for the fifty-year-old worker. If we assume that the fifty-year-old worker has been earning $50,000 for the last twenty years of his or her life, we should hope that they have accumulated at least $250,000 in net worth. At fifty years old, an individual should have been working long enough to have at least a substantial amount saved in a retirement account and have a home free from all debt obligations. We should at least give the older and wiser among us the benefit of the doubt that they have had plenty of time to make mistakes, learn from them, and then eventually make corrective financial decisions. In fact, we could make a strong argument that the fifty-year-old worker should have plenty more saved. Assuming that the fifty-year-old worker has saved 15% of his or her pre-taxed earnings over the last twenty years and put them into a portfolio with a company 3% of employee earnings contribution match and underlying investments averaging 6% a year, the portfolio will have a value of over $340,000! This value does not even include the values of other assets that would contribute to their net worth.

Account Values for the Next 20 Years			
Year	Employee Salary	Employee Contribution	Employer Matching Contribution	Total Account Value
1	50,000.00	7,500.00	1,500.00	9,297.93
2	50,000.00	7,500.00	1,500.00	19,169.34
3	50,000.00	7,500.00	1,500.00	29,649.59
4	50,000.00	7,500.00	1,500.00	40,776.24
5	50,000.00	7,500.00	1,500.00	52,589.16
6	50,000.00	7,500.00	1,500.00	65,130.67
7	50,000.00	7,500.00	1,500.00	78,445.72
8	50,000.00	7,500.00	1,500.00	92,582.01
9	50,000.00	7,500.00	1,500.00	107,590.20
10	50,000.00	7,500.00	1,500.00	123,524.06
11	50,000.00	7,500.00	1,500.00	140,440.68
12	50,000.00	7,500.00	1,500.00	158,400.69
13	50,000.00	7,500.00	1,500.00	177,468.42
14	50,000.00	7,500.00	1,500.00	197,712.22
15	50,000.00	7,500.00	1,500.00	219,204.60
16	50,000.00	7,500.00	1,500.00	242,022.60
17	50,000.00	7,500.00	1,500.00	266,247.95
18	50,000.00	7,500.00	1,500.00	291,967.47
19	50,000.00	7,500.00	1,500.00	319,273.32
20	50,000.00	7,500.00	1,500.00	348,263.32

We Don't Believe Wealth Is Within Our Reach

The previous example should show that it is not too difficult to build a decent net worth over time and that the formula in *The Millionaire Next Door* is not unrealistic. Although many variables—such as taxes and inflation—were not accounted for in the assumed portfolio, neither was the possibility that over twenty years the income of the worker increases. In other words, the example only assumes that the 15%, plus 3% employer matching contributions were only made from $50,000. We should hope that there was an increase in salary over twenty years. Hence, there would be in increase in the amount accumulated.

What if in addition to the worker's retirement contributions, at the age of thirty-five, he or she had decided to purchase a home using a fifteen-year fixed-rate mortgage? If our worker would have stayed in this home after the initial purchase, wouldn't that home be paid off once the worker reaches fifty years old, assuming no additional loans were mortgaged on the property? Wouldn't this add even more to his or her net worth? So, haven't we proven that over fifteen years, with just two investment vehicles, one can build a huge net worth? Given this detail, there is no reason, other than the restrictions that the worker has probably put on herself, why her net worth couldn't have met the prediction of Stanley and Danko's formula.

What about a dual income family? What would be the net worth of a household with two workers starting at age thirty, both making $50,000 annually? Assuming that we can just double the supposed net worth of each worker, they should have accumulated a net worth of at least $500,000 and have a paid-off home after only twenty years of working. Is this really unreasonable? Of course not, and remember that this example used only very conservative estimates and only two retirement vehicles. But, how many fifty-year-olds have amassed this type of net worth? How many dual-income families do you know that are working towards amassing this type of net worth? If we live in a home that is paid for, and continually choose to save a percentage of our income as our income grows, is there any reason why we can't retire way before sixty years old?

While it may seem, on the surface, that the only way to have the net worth described by Stanley and Danko is to purchase and pay off a home, which in many cases is ideal, we have shown that retirement savings (neglecting inflation) that takes advantage of an employer match can get us at least to a respectable net worth. So, what barriers exist to prevent us from doing so? I submit that with the exception of rare cases, the barriers that prevent us from doing so are all self-inflicted.

We have to discover for ourselves where we fall short in the journey to amass net worth. It is within reach for many of us if we allow it to be.

At your current income and age, where should you be financially?

$$\frac{Pretax\ annual\ income\ \times\ age}{10} = net\ worth$$

Partly because of my age, but mainly because of my financial mistakes, my net worth will not accurately reflect Stanley and Danko's formula. My mortgage balance in itself is still over $160,000, so my net worth is far less than what it should be, though, it should be far greater than what it is. According to this formula, my net worth *should* be $68,000 x 30/10 = $204,000. Is this unreasonable for my age? Maybe, because I have not always earned $68,000 annually, but had I saved 20% of my earned income over the past thirteen years and had more equity in my home, I'd have a net worth of at least $88,000.

Many of us fall short of our true financial entitlement because of the simple ignorance of not knowing where to start. Others of us fall into the trap of living beyond our means, or spending all that we earn, because we're somehow plagued with the thought that *we can't spend it when we're dead.* Perhaps the latter is true, but what happens when we actually do outlive our money? Or even if we don't outlive our money, what happens to our dependents who are left behind to cover our financial burdens when we are dead? If we don't care about ourselves, shouldn't we unselfishly care about them?

The income that we spend the majority of our lives working to get should not only pay bills and give us a comfortable standard of living now, but it should also work to give us freedom of choice, be it now, or later in our lives when we may long for it most. If all of our earnings are continually tied up in things, and not working towards building our net worth, we will be able to only pay bills, if we're lucky—we'll never have the financial freedom of choice. If our houses, cars, credit cards, student loans, and other debts are not paid off once we reach forty or fifty years old, and if we have not accumulated the funds to pay them off, we will unfortunately, but realistically have no other choice but to continue working way into what should be our golden years.

We Don't Believe Wealth Is Within Our Reach

Not focusing on financial freedom will hurt us in the end. We can't always rely on a company for our financial security. What would happen if the company had a bad year? Would we have the flexibility to recover from a company downsizing or a lay-off? Would we have the financial freedom to wait out a year while waiting to be hired at another place of employment?

There has to come a time when we can no longer blame our jobs or the government for our own mistakes. Every time we purchase things instead of contributing to our net worth or financial freedom, we make an unconscious decision to not build wealth, but prevent it. Like this chapter's example has shown, wealth is within reach for many, if not all of us.

Let there be no mistake about it, however. The less money that we make, the harder it is to accumulate wealth. Not everyone earns $50,000 a year. In fact, the median household income for America is still around $45,000. But that shouldn't deter us from saving. Or more importantly, a "meager" wage shouldn't stop us from taking the appropriate steps to earn even more now so that we don't have to work twice as hard in the future. We have to let go of the excuses and start building wealth, because once again, it is within reach if we make wise financial choices early in our lives.

We Don't Believe Wealth Is Within Our Reach

Chapter 3

We Don't Reflect on Where We Stand

When we turn thirty years old, we are half-way to the age of sixty. In other words, we are halfway to an age at which we should be able to retire. I mean, why should we not stop working after thirty or more years of servitude, if we desire? Why should we wait until we are able to collect social security before we consider ourselves retired?

The majority of workers have been working and earning wages for many years, and consequently, those workers are very close to an ideal retirement age. Yet, many of them are very far off from becoming wealthy, despite receiving a lifetime of earnings. It is sad that many of us will live our lives without being able to live comfortably in our "golden years"; although I would argue that this comfort is well within reach for nearly everyone, assuming they minimize wealth preventing decisions early enough to recover from them.

Perhaps the attitude of the majority is of the contrary, that wealth was never possible for them because of meager wages, or a lack of educational opportunities, or because of poor investments. But I would argue that this same majority has had a lifetime of opportunity or are living a life in which the opportunity is still available to accumulate wealth. However, before we know it, we are going to wake up and realize that we blew it, having no one to blame but ourselves. We're going to realize that we have been working all of our lives, but don't have an asset to show for it with the exception of maybe a nice new car or grand home that we're still making payments on. And when we die, after all of our hard years of continuous working and minimum savings, we'll just end up passing the "assets" off to our heirs so that they can worry about how to pay the debts off. Hopefully, we'll at least have a life insurance policy so that our dependents won't have to worry too much about paying down those "assets."

Most of our problems that prevent us from building wealth result from our own doings. We choose to have huge amounts of debt even though we have minimum savings and no prospect of retirement income. And after we accumulate such debts, we then tell ourselves that we don't have enough money to save, or we simply put our savings on hold until we feel comfortable paying down other things. Some of us are only one or two paychecks away from financial distress. I know I was for a long time and am currently fighting to stay ahead.

How We Prevent Wealth

Even if we are not teetering on the edge of financial distress, many of us are stuck in jobs that we don't like so that we can pay for things that we bought but can't afford. There is nothing that we can do about it, because we unfortunately have too many bills to pay. According to a study, *I Can't Get No...Job Satisfaction, That Is*, conducted by the Conference Board and released in 2010, many people are fed up and dissatisfied with their jobs, yet they are not making any progress to do something about it or creating the leverage to simply quit. The study found that Americans' job satisfaction fell to a new record low in 2009. It shows that only 45.3% of people who had a job were satisfied with their work in 2009. When the study started in 1987, over 61% of Americans were satisfied with their job. Despite the results of this study, we are obviously not fed up enough if we are not actively seeking the financial knowledge to one day set up our own financial utopia. Instead of working towards being free, we are creating our own financial doom by failing ourselves.

If we don't earn to save, and save to prepare, how can we ever fully enjoy life? Why do we long for a life as if we are children who are dependent on parents? If our parents were to decide that the "bank of Mom and Dad" has gone bankrupt, wouldn't we have to find another source of dependency? Similarly, if our employers decided they could no longer afford to pay us; wouldn't we have to find another source of dependency? Why should we settle on earning an "allowance?" Why should we choose to be under the constraints of our bosses just as our children are constrained under us? Why should we live a life of servitude up until we finally die? Where is the freedom in that? Shouldn't we at least work towards our own independence? It has taken me until now to see life for what it is for the majority of people. They live, they work, and they die. We can do better. We can strive to live, work, live, and then die.

My biggest revelation and scare is that my entire life will be consumed by working for wages; I do not want to spend my entire adult life working—and I don't understand why anyone would want that. We can instead look forward to the day when we no longer have to get up out of our warm cozy beds because we *have* to work. It would be better to have to get up out of our warm cozy beds because we *want* to work, and if we don't get out of our beds, we shouldn't have to be "penalized" by a reduction in pay or other negative consequences. This is the freedom that I seek. This is the freedom that we all can seek.

How We Prevent Wealth

Many of our days are consumed with a mandatory structure, leaving us no room to do what we truly want to do. In a standard work day, we may spend up to ten hours working. In the remaining hours, we have to transition to and from our home, use an hour or more in total of our day eating, and eight hours sleeping, if we're lucky. Can you see that this leaves us only five hours a day for other things such as spending time with family or recreation? Depending on how demanding our families are, this kind of schedule does not leave much time for self. This limits the number of golf games played, the number of television shows watched, the number of hours spent reading a good book, or time doing whatever it is that *we* truly enjoy. We live, we work, and we finally die. Why should we accept this as a way of life when we really don't have to?

We will never be free unless we realize how we constrain ourselves. Why should we be constrained to our jobs—because we always have to pay bills? I reject this line of reasoning. Even if we do desire to work, why should we not at the very least be able to minimize the hours that we *choose* to work so that we may maximize our time for family and self? Shouldn't we be able to take two weeks of vacation when we want to, or spend any day we choose playing golf or some other sport in beautiful weather? Is this too much to ask for? Shouldn't we deserve such a privilege after working for thirty or forty years? Why does this lifestyle have to be preserved for just the rich and famous? Shouldn't we all desire this—true retirement, true wealth, true financial freedom? Well, the only way to reach such a goal is to consistently work at it and be aware of how not to put obstacles in front of the goals we set.

The younger we are, the better we can take advantage of opportunities and recover from failed mistakes. Why should we spend the years when our money should be working for us, paying on debts that work against us? The older we are, the less time we have for our money to work for us, so there is especially no reason for us to procrastinate and continue to make horrible financial decisions.

We have to ask ourselves what we are doing to prevent our wealth. This realization is as important in knowing how we accumulate wealth. Imagine realizing this after forty years of working. Imagine making it to sixty years old and realizing that even though we've worked for our entire adult life, we still can't stop because of a series of financial decisions that we've never overcome.

I accept the notion that all of our lives can be spent accumulating wealth, and that we all deserve it. We just have to know where we tend to go wrong financially, and exchange these bad choices for wealth-accumulation decisions. Only then can we take a turn on them. Our financial freedom is within our reach, but just like anything, it takes a strong willingness to sacrifice and delay gratification. Most importantly, we have to hurry to eliminate the poor attitudes that created the financial mistakes we have made and put them behind us.

The accumulation of our "small," bad decisions are critical to laying out our futures—they have huge negative impacts that affect many different aspects of our lives. Our poor decisions affect how long we will eventually work, the time that we have to enjoy family, and the time that we have to spend on our own interests. We do not realize our horrible spending habits or decisions. We do not realize that we prevent wealth.

We Don't Reflect on Where We Stand

Chapter 4

We Don't Live on a Budget

We have all heard how important it is to budget our monthly income, yet many of us shrug it off. In our minds we have valid and legitimate reasons for doing so.

In some cases, we just get overwhelmed with the requirements and the time that it takes. One would think that developing a budget is easy to do. But then again, liken it to anything that takes practice. For example, imagine if we were a child who has to learn how to tie a shoe for the first time. Would this not be a difficult task? While it is a simple task for the child who has been tying shoes for years, it probably would not come easy to us, the first timer.

Indeed, it may take us many tries before we finally "get it." The adult (or teen) who attempts proficiency at a budget measures their tries in months. In other words, while a child can try multiple attempts in one day to learn how to tie a shoe, the adult trying to manage a budget may wait one month before he can start over after realizing that he messed things up.

I can remember when I first started my Microsoft Excel spreadsheet in an attempt to draft up my budget about eight years ago. In that year alone, I probably changed my monthly budget about fifty times—even multiple times in a session after spending about two hours staring at my spreadsheet, hypothesizing and evaluating how things should shift.

In order to become proficient at a budget, we have to continually work at it, and do so until we persevere. I'm sure that the majority of people who have become wealthy did not do it overnight. They most likely did so by planning and setting goals that were monitored and measured using a continually-tweaked-until-proficient budget.

Budgeting is not as easy as everyone makes it sound, psychologically at least. However, if we are to grow financially, we have to learn the mechanics of establishing a budget. A budget consists of simply knowing where our money is going. A budget helps to ensure that we don't spend more money than we have coming in. If it's too late because we are already spending much more than we're bringing in, a budget allows us to see where there is flexibility so we can make adjustments and curb our spending.

Budgeting Is Like Apple Pie

In the end, a budget is much like, say, a pie. Let's go with a budget being an apple pie, but of course at the same time, everyone wants their slice of it. Yet, before we can distribute pie out to everyone, we have to first know how big our pie is. We can only really know how many people will ultimately get a slice by determining its size. And because we are the ones cutting it, we can decide to give each person more or less.

However, we also want some of our pie. So we have to think of clever ways to maximum our piece of the pie. This can come in the form of eating a couple of slices now or eating large slices later. Better yet, we can do both as long as we are selfish enough to feed ourselves first. So the real question becomes, "how would we maximize our slice(s)?"

To answer this question, we would need to:

1. Realize how large our pie is (Calculate our monthly income)
2. Determine how many slices are distributed to everyone else (Determine how much we spend on monthly bills)
3. Determine how many pieces we sneak off the crust (Track our daily expenses)

Realizing How Large Our Pie Is (Calculate Our Monthly Income after Taxes)

Thankfully, calculating our monthly income is straight forward for many of us. Most salary workers already know what their monthly income is because it is usually fixed. Likewise, many people will know how large their pie is because, well, they will usually be the one who made it.

However, this step will probably pose a problem for anyone who is not on a fixed monthly income or is brought pies of various sizes by other people as gifts. But, never fear. We would just pick a very conservative estimate. For example, if one month we make $2,500 and the next month we make $2,000, we would base our budget on the lowest amount. Anything over $2,000 should be saved in a separate account. This way we won't be surprised if we can't make bill payments one month if they total more than $2,000.

Knowing this information is one third of our battle. Once our monthly income is determined, we would write it down somewhere, be it on paper, in a spreadsheet, or in the crust of a pie. We should just do it.

Determining How Many Slices Are Distributed to Everyone Else (Determine How Much We Spend on Monthly Bills)

Once we determine our monthly pre-taxed income, and have written it down, we need to find out who is taking from it. Or, in keeping with our metaphor, we need to know how many slices of pie we are giving and who usually ends up taking how much.

The best way to perform this feat is to lay out all of our monthly bills—credit cards, mortgage, auto loans, charity, and so forth. After these bills are gathered, we would write these down under our total monthly income determined from step 1. If the amounts are variable (changes frequently every month), just as in the case of the varied paycheck, we would simply estimate a monthly payment. But, here we should choose the least conservative amount. For example, if our electric bill is $230 one month, but $300 another month, we would just choose $300 as that monthly amount.

After all of our bills are determined and written down, we should then subtract them from our monthly income. This is the point where we will freak out, be indifferent, or be content. What remains of course is what's left over for us and our family. But, in terms of pie, we should freak out if what was left over after distributing to others was not a very large slice (for seconds, or thirds, or fifths).

Next, we should determine an estimate for the amount of monthly discretionary expenditures. We should determine how much we spend on household products, groceries, movie subscriptions, and so on. These amounts should also be written down. This is our first slice of pie that we are receiving from what's remaining.

How's that pie looking right now? Do you have any remaining? If so, what remains is your pleasure slice—the slice that satisfies all of those late night cravings and that supplements your vanilla ice cream. In terms of personal finances, this remainder is what is left that is not accounted for by someone else. Still, before we package this remaining pie so that it can be stored and eaten at a later time, we should let it lay on the countertop, aroma still circulating in the air.

Determining How Many Pieces That We Sneak off the Crust (Track Our Daily Expenses)

This I would argue is the hardest one-third of our battle. It is difficult at best to track our daily expenses if we are not accustomed to it. Likewise, it is difficult to control how often we should sneak pieces of our pie's crust as it lay on the countertop if we have a habit of bingeing. All that we would end up knowing is one day we had a pie, and the next day we didn't.

If we are not aware of how many pieces we sneak, we can later end up with no pie at all. If we did have to give out a second helping to someone because they were, say, calling in a favor, we couldn't. This is why we must maximize our leftovers and accumulate them for a midnight craving. We must control and track these "crust sneaks," or the daily expenses that "eat" away at our discretionary funds.

We have to know which daily expenses are getting in the way of our maximum pie slice. Is it a coffee and a bagel every morning, dining out every weekend, purchasing movies or makeup? Whatever they are, we have to be aware of them. Remember, think maximum pie slices.

There are many ways to track our daily expenses, though; we just have to find which one works best for us. Traditionally speaking, we can simply save every receipt and categorize things ourselves. However, in the modern age, programs such as Intuit's Quicken or other software programs are great for tracking expenses after having saved the receipt for such an input, or we can simply let the program take over by downloading the most current data from our bank accounts. Even further, some banks are beginning to categorize spending for their members. And most recently, Web programs such as Intuit's Mint.com, is ridiculously awesome at tracking and categorizing expenses—and it's free.

Once again, tracking our expenses is important to maximum slices of pie for us and for others if, or when, a second helping is requested (think of the second helpings as debt collectors calling for more than the minimum payments). So there you have it, our budget is—like apple pie. To not *prevent wealth* is to maximize our slice of pie.

A Simple and Flexible Way to Budget

In its most basic form, a budget should not only direct where our pay goes within the constraints that we set, it should also be efficient, and realistically work. There are several "formulas" regarding how to set a budget, but they will never work if we are not diligent about keeping within our constraints. While it takes discipline to keep to our budgets, it's only as hard as we make it.

My recommendation for a budget is one that has every dollar coming into the home, consistently going into one of several main categories. One of the main categories, discretionary spending, has subcategories that we should be free to shift around if necessary. This plan is pretty flexible and is shown in the following example. For simplicity, a monthly after-tax income of $2500 is assumed.

Category 1: Retirement. This is always first. Period. There are several guidelines that say 10–15%, but the best guideline is to save as much as we can in this category commensurate with a desired retirement monthly income, because the more and the longer we save here, the better our lifestyle in retirement. Let's go with 15%, $375 per month in this case. So $375 from $2500 would leave $2125.

Category 2: Emergency Savings. Here we should consistently save enough in a liquid account such as a certificate of deposit, basic, or money market savings account to be able to weather any storms. A guideline is about six months' worth of living expenses. Living expenses are those that are required to absolutely survive in the event of a job lost. If we work in a volatile industry, we may need to save more than six months' worth of living expenses. When we are comfortable with our amount, we can stop contributing here and shift the money to another category. For our example, let's go with $125 a month, putting us at $2,000 remaining.

Category 3: Long-term Savings. Our long-term savings should be consistent with any long-term goals. For example, if we want to be able to put 20% down on a home in about five years (assume a $100,000 home price) we should be saving $333.33 per month to save $20,000. If a long-term goal is to get out of debt, then we should focus on instead putting our long-term "savings" towards our debts. For example, if we have $20,000 in debt, we should put $333.33 a month towards this amount to be out of debt in about five years. This puts us at $1666.67 remaining for short-term goals and discretionary spending.

Category 4: Short-term Savings. This category is established to help us purchase things without using credit. We determine how much it should be. We'll be surprised at how quickly it adds up if we consistently put money towards this category. A monthly amount of $166.67 is a pretty good amount that adds to $2,000 over one year and still leaves us $1,500 a month for the last category.

Category 5: Living Expenses and Discretionary Spending. Once the previous four categories are taken care of, now we can decide how to live within our means of $1,500 using subcategories. An example can be:

$600 Rent

$400 Groceries

$300 Utilities

$100 Household items

$100 Entertainment

$1500 Total

In the end, we're left with $000.00 at the end of the month with savings and expenses taken care of. The next fight is just learning to stay within our subcategories as best we can. The subcategories can be flexible. If we overspend on groceries in the same amount that we underspend on household, our discretionary spending ultimately balances out (we just have to be conscious not to do this very often). Of course the numbers presented in this example are only guidelines, as we only know our particular situation; the process is what's important.

Tracking within a Budget

Having a budget is a good thing; it's a very good choice, and it puts us a step above the many people who fail to use one. It puts a restriction on our spending in a giving category and in theory allows us to save money by doing so. But what's fundamentally more important than having a budget is being able to stay within our constraints, or at least be able to evaluate why we didn't stay within them during a past period so that we'd do better in the next budget period.

A common problem is that despite our good intentions, many of our budgets still consistently fail. Perhaps it is because we simple forgot about a few transactions that we've made over the weekend or a check that we wrote several weeks ago. So the question is how do we at least try to prevent what seems so inevitable?

There are several ways to at least mitigate this problem whether it is done traditionally by pencil and paper or in the more modern era of electronics. Here are two great suggestions:

1) **The envelope system:** An envelope system is where we place cash in an envelope per category at the beginning of the month. For example, we would take several envelopes and label one of them groceries, another

as household, another as entertainment, and so on, and place in them a certain amount. For instance, let's say we put $500 in an envelope for groceries. The $500 would be our monthly budget for this specific item. We would only spend from this envelope, and if before the end of the month we find ourselves with no money remaining, we would not spend any further; we would improvise to make a couple of meals with what we already have in the house.

2) **The receipt and enter system:** This system works best for me. I use Intuit's Quicken for my personal finance tracking. I've also used other software in the past such as the defunct Microsoft's Money. If this doesn't' work well, we can use free personal software programs on the Web such as Mint.com. All are good and very efficient programs once we learn their sometimes cumbersome techniques to set up our budgets in them. Once set up, every time a purchase is made, whether it is an over-the-counter purchase or payment by check, the transaction should be manually entered in the software. For every transaction, we would keep the receipt in our wallet or purse, and at the end of the day, we would manually enter our transactions in our program. Despite the fact that most of the software automatically downloads our bank's transactions; manual entry is our own backup to protect

ourselves from a bank's potentially incorrect or delayed postings, which can occur. This process avoids the pending or floating check problem that deceives us into thinking that we have more money than we actually have.

Conclusion

Learning the basics of budgeting is fundamental to having a successful financial plan. Without establishing one, it may be difficult to begin the next basics that follow: saving and investing for specific things in our future. The earlier in our careers that we understand budgets and stick to the constraints within it, the better we may be able to avoid the traps of living on credit and beyond our means.

Chapter 5

We Don't Educate Ourselves

It seems quite obvious to me that our best chance to create wealth is by earning money and saving some of it through various investment vehicles. In fact, we have a better chance of building wealth this way than receiving an inheritance, winning the lottery, or receiving a multi-million dollar contract as an entertainer or sports star. What's unique about this observation is that the latter four are based mainly on luck or an extraordinary talent, which many of us unfortunately do not have. But nearly all of us have an earning potential, and this earning potential allows us to earn, save, and grow our money. However, in order to tap the full potential of our earnings, we must take advantage of education.

Two types of education are important in building wealth. First there is a formal education, which is obtained by attending school. Second there is an informal education, which is received out of school. Either one will do if applied correctly. Both types of education directly reflect how much our money will grow over a lifetime. In fact, our incomes are our greatest wealth-building assets. So knowing this, and reflecting on it, why do we choose to not further our education so that we may build our wealth overtime? Let's first talk about the formal education.

Formal Education

No one should dare tell you that it's *easy* to become wealthy on meager wages such as the federally-mandated minimum wage. It's a lie. If your wages are so low that you are constantly fighting to pay the next bill, having a sufficient amount of money remaining to grow to a substantial sum is nearly impossible. It can be done, but it will not be easy. And this assumes that you have plenty of time for your investments to grow. And even so, there is no doubt about it that the higher your pay, the easier it is to save money that can be used to continuously max out retirement accounts or invest in opportunities when they present themselves. Yet, too many of us do not understand the correlation between higher education and higher pay. Instead of continually pursuing knowledge, we become content and consequently accept far less in pay than we can receive if we were to continue educating ourselves.

The truth will always hold that *applied knowledge is power.* Consequently, by furthering our education, and therefore our knowledge, we make ourselves more marketable and we challenge ourselves to create ideas—

ideas that may one day turn a product or a service into substantial earnings. We become viable members of society. We can command higher pay.

So why is it that we have so many excuses not to further our education? Where is the push or the self-motivation? Why do we let so many things get in our way? These days, both a formal and an informal education are easy to obtain. We have at our disposals: military scholarships, federal aid and grants, and private scholarships and grants, if eligible. Even some of the organizations for which we work practically subsidize our education through tuition reimbursement programs; it is in their best interest to do so, because it keeps a more knowledgeable worker in the organization. So once again, why do we have so many excuses?

Our excuses are just a series of detrimental complaints. We complain that there is not enough time in our daily schedules or we were never good enough in school. We also complain that school is too expensive, we don't like school, or that school is just not important. However, the truth is that there is plenty of time if we make school a priority because it *is* important. There is no better time to challenge ourselves in a particular subject than when we are adults—who by the way are responsible for challenging our own children or peers. And as far as not liking school or saying that it is not important, it's important that we do like it unless we have a better plan to create and maximize our incomes by some other means.

So what are our options for a formal education? As we all know, there is the traditional classroom setting and there are now plenty of colleges and universities that have extended their programs via distant learning. And if we don't like the distant learning, some colleges offer entire weekend-based degree programs where a degree is earned by taking classes locally on the weekends. This means that we are allowed increased flexibility to attend school more than we have ever been in the past. Yet, we do not take advantage of education.

Studies conducted as recently as 2010 by the U.S. Census Bureau have concluded that adults with only a high school education earn approximately $1.2 million dollars over an average lifespan. However, adults with a bachelor's degree earn approximately $2.1 million dollars over an average lifespan, and those adults with a master's degree earn over $3.4 million dollars over an average lifespan. So, by looking at education as a measurement alone, an adult with a master's degree is already ahead of an adult with only a high-school education by a lifetime earnings of $2.2

million dollars. Although these are average numbers, and they vary among the different educational disciplines, the numbers prove the importance of higher formal education.

When Is the High Cost of Tuition Worth Its Price?

Although we have seen how important it is to obtain a formal education, we still have to be smart about our decisions when picking a college. This is where the intuition should kick in. Just as I presented data that shows that an adult with a master's degree will earn more than an adult with only a high school diploma, someone can present a study that shows that an adult attending an Ivy League school will earn more than an adult who does not. Additionally, someone can also present a study showing that someone who attends a private university earns more on average than someone who attends a public university.

What we have to realize is that the choice we make when we ultimately choose a school may help us *prevent wealth,* rather than build wealth in the end. For example, how many friends do we know with degrees that they went deeply into debt to get, but for a career that doesn't even pay annually the amount of debt that was used to receive the degree?

Our environment puts such a premium on a "quality degree" that it leads to what I would call, irrational spending on college tuition. Some people attend private colleges based on the name and not the educational system itself. In some cases the education you can receive at a private university is similar to the education you can receive at a state school, except that you may pay ten times more for it. Both schools often use the same textbooks, which should beg the question, "What does a quality degree entail?" In some cases the best answer may be the networking that has the *potential* of landing a career with a higher paying salary. For example, the tuition at the school where I received my graduate business degree cost me a little more than $19,000. At this price, I learned every standard business course that is taught at any college; yet there are colleges charging up to $100,000 for their business degree program.

So, what makes the extra $85,000 worth it? Is it because of the perceived prestige of those universities? If so, we should really ask ourselves how much we are willing to pay for this prestige. Before committing to a university, we must understand what our educational goals are. We have to determine whether our goals are to simply learn the curriculum, to learn the curriculum from world-renowned professors, or to learn the curriculum from world-renowned professors while having the capability to network in circles of "Who's Who around Wall Street?" I'm fine with simply learning the curriculum, as I have no desire to work on Wall Street.

There has to be a fine line drawn between earning a degree that gives us a higher earnings potential, and one that leaves us in debt beyond what is necessary to obtain that higher earnings potential. Traditionally, personal finance gurus tell us that debt is good for at least two things: buying a house and paying for school. But where do we set the limits for such thoughts? Should a person who aspires to be an elementary school teacher, whose national median salary is approximately $45,000[i], use $100,000 worth of student loans to pay for an undergraduate degree? At what anticipated salary should we conclude that it is not worth going heavily in debt for?

The Case for an Average Paid School Teacher

Let us assume that we are a future elementary school teacher, and it will take us five years to obtain an undergraduate degree at a private university where five years of tuition amounts to $75,000. Let us further assume that we obtain $24,500 in student scholarships, leaving us with a total of $50,500 to be paid with various student loans. The breakdown of such a payment schedule can be approximated at the *College Board* Web site.

We'll assume that we will borrow $4,600 per year for five years using a subsidized Federal Stafford Loan. Furthermore, we'll assume that we'll borrow $5500 per year for five years using a Perkins Loan. Using these two loans to cover our $50,500 amounts to $542 per month for the next ten years! And this particular example is based on only a 5.6% and a 6.8% annual percentage rate, respectively.

Subsidized Federal Stafford Loan Borrowing Summary	
Principal you have borrowed or expect to borrow	$23,000
Total interest to be repaid (interest accrued during in-school and grace periods is paid by the federal government)	$7,090
Total amount of principal and interest to be repaid	$30,090
Monthly repayment (if less than $ 50, a minimum monthly payment of $ 50 would be required).	$251

This analysis assumes you qualify for a subsidized Federal Stafford Loan and would not be required to pay interest on your loans while in school. The analysis assumes an annual interest rate of 5.60 % and that you will repay your loan over a ten-year period following graduation in 120 equal monthly installments. For purposes of this analysis, dependent student loan limits were used.

Perkins Loan Borrowing Summary	
Principal you have borrowed or expect to borrow	$27,500
Total interest to be repaid	$7,502
Total amount of principal and interest to be repaid	$35,002
Monthly repayment	$292

This analysis assumes you qualify for a Perkins loan on the basis of demonstrated financial need. Interest payments would be deferred while you are in college, graduate or professional school. The analysis assumes an annual interest rate of 5.0 % and that you will repay your loan over a ten-year period following graduation in 120 equal monthly installments.

Consolidated Borrowing Summary	
Grand total principal you have borrowed or expect to borrow	$50,500
Total interest to be repaid	$14,592
Total amount of principal and interest to be repaid	$65,092
Combined monthly repayment	$542

This analysis combines your Stafford, Perkins, and Other Loans into a consolidated summary, based on the above information.

Will a $542 monthly payment for the next ten years be manageable for someone who makes only $45,000 a year, or approximately $4167 per month before taxes? It all depends on someone's situation. Knowing that the majority of student loan holders see this as "good debt," it is not likely to be a priority to pay off. It is more likely that the loan holder will buy a car with a $500 monthly payment, and then a house with a thirty-year fixed monthly payment around $1,000 instead, adding to the total amount of debt owed. These are not unreasonable assumptions for the average American. Two thousand dollars in monthly debt doesn't leave much for savings if we are only earning $4,500 per month, considering that another $1,500 or more will end up going towards utilities, groceries, household items, and other miscellaneous expenses. But the real question becomes, is it even necessary to pay a total of over $65,000 in loans for an education if we can earn the same type of degree that will land us the same annual salary by attending a less expensive college? I would argue no, but it is something that each of us should at least consider.

So what's the point? The point is that we should earn a degree to the extent that it will maximize our future earning potential, and depending on our goals, it may be best to do it at the lowest cost. In most cases it is our work ethic that will set us apart from the competition in the end, not the ridiculous amount of money that we have spent for our degree. If we are idiots in our field, despite our "premium" degree, we many end up without a job, and the only thing to show for our degree will be our massive lifetime student loan payments.

Furthermore, it should be noted that a college degree only increases our chances—it does not guarantee—that we will earn more money. So why go into so much debt, *preventing wealth*, right off the bat, even before we begin a career? By all means, we should attend the best college that we can, but within the bounds of a reasonable price that is relative to our future earnings.

Don't Underestimate the Value of Informal Education.

Even if we finally obtain a degree, or choose not to obtain one at all, our education should not stop. This is where the informal education comes in. An informal education is obtained through extensive reading, learning from various educational sources, and having a genuine interest in something that invokes our wiliness to learn more. Whether the informal education is obtained from spending countless hours on the Internet reading about a particular subject of interest, or working and continually learning the "ins and outs" of an automobile workshop, *learning* is the key and has the possibility of converting our education into wealth.

My knowledge in personal finance did not come by way of college courses, nor did it come by way of a certification. In fact, I was disappointed when I learned that my graduate studies did not touch on the subject enough. But this did not stop me from reading news articles about personal finance, borrowing books from the library about the subject, or finding people with common interests so that I could discuss it with them. The extent to which my efforts will help me to build wealth remain to be seen; but the point is that my knowledge in personal finance comes purely from informal sources.

There are many people without a college degree who have become wealthy, but they did not do so by being content with only their high school education, to be sure. Perhaps countless hours spent on the Internet learning a subject by reading blogs inspired someone to take their knowledge and start a business that produced an income that eventually accumulated into wealth. Perhaps the automobile mechanic, who was inspired by his or her interest, earned a certification in the field, which translated into earning more income to be saved towards accumulating wealth. Whatever the case, whether formal or informal, an education leads to an increase in our earning potential. This concept should not be ignored.

In many cases, an informal education's only cost is time. If we have any interest at all, a good library could be our conduit for this information. A good public library has a wealth of information: documentary DVDs, computers with Internet access, audio CDs, magazines, encyclopedias, and topic-specific books. We just have to find a way to get to the library and take the time to explore it.

One thing is for certain, if we do not take the time to educate ourselves, we will most likely miss out on the potential to earn greater incomes over a lifetime. We'll never know whether or not we might have earned more if we never give ourselves a chance.

We Don't Educate Ourselves

Chapter 6

We Set Ineffective Financial Goals

It is great to have goals, and it is better to have a goal than to have none at all. However, so many of our goals are either ineffective or unrealistic. Many of them are derived from "cookie-cutter" ideas such as save 15% towards retirement, save $2,000 a year for your children's college, or save six months' worth of living expenses in an emergency account. Like I said, these goals are better than having none at all, but the question is whether these goals are right for every one of us. To be effective, a financial goal must be: measurable, such that it has a specific timeline and amount; purposeful, such that it is working towards something; and realistic, such that it is within our earning capacity.

An Ineffective Retirement Savings Approach

If we earn $4,000 in monthly pre-tax income, should we follow a rule of thumb that says to save 15% towards retirement? Will this be enough? Do we have enough information at this point to make an informed judgment? The answer is no. Shouldn't we factor other things into this recommendation such as our current age, our current monthly income upon which this percentage is based, the age that we desire to retire, and the amount of income desired in retirement? Does a thirty-year-old person who makes $100,000 in annual income, but has yet to start saving for retirement need to save at the same rate as someone who is forty years old, making the same amount of money, but also has yet to start saving for retirement?

If we save 15% of a $4,000 monthly income at the age of thirty years old, this would amount to a monthly savings of $600. Will this be enough for retirement? We will be saving, which is good, but the question will never be effectively answered until further information is considered—it should all depend on what we want our desired income to be at retirement.

For now, let us see what $600 a month will yield. (The resulting information can be found using an online retirement income calculator such as the one found on Bankrate.com.) Saving $600 per month will allow us to save $7200 per year. Let us assume that we decide to save this money into a tax-deferred retirement account such as a traditional IRA, and in turn, we want to be able to have a retirement income stream from age sixty-five until age ninety. Next, we'll assume that we are in a 25% marginal tax bracket now, will be in a 15% marginal tax bracket throughout retirement, inflation will stay at a rate of 2%, and that our money will grow tax-deferred at a rate of 6% annually. After doing the calculations, we will have an approximate retirement income stream of $4588 monthly (or $2294 in today's dollars) for twenty-five years, after taxes and inflation. Not bad, right?

What if we decided to wait until we were forty years old to begin saving this same 15%, assuming that we made the same income and were subject to the same tax brackets and inflation? Would the 15% retirement income rule of thumb be sufficient enough to live for twenty-five years in a comfortable retirement? Not really, especially if one "retires" with other debts such as a mortgage. Saving at the same rate of 15% would only yield $2259 per month for twenty-five years, a value equivalent to $1377 in today's dollars after adjusting for assumed taxes and inflation.

Clearly, we have to not only set a goal to retire, but evaluate how much money our investment will possibly yield in retirement. It should be obvious by these calculations that the later we begin saving, the more we need to adjust our retirement savings rate. In other words, 15% may be good for person A, but an inadequate percentage for person B, depending on their definition of financial freedom.

Retirement Income Results for a $7200 Annual Contribution for Thirty-five Years.	
Starting Balance	$0
Annual Contribution	$7,200
Current Age	30
Age of Retirement	65
Years of Retirement	25
Rate of Return Before Retirement	6.00%
Rate of Return During Retirement	6.00%
Current Tax Rate	25.00%
Retirement Tax Rate	15.00%
Expected Rate of Inflation	2.00%
Is This Savings Tax Deferred?	yes
Increase Annual Deposit with Inflation?	no
Total Contributions	**$252,000**
Savings Total Before Taxes	$850,470
Savings Total After Taxes	$722,900
Value of Savings in Today's Dollars	**$361,470**
Savings Can Provide	
Income Before Taxes	$5,397 per month
Income After Taxes	$4,588 per month
Value of Income in Today's Dollars (With 2.00% Annual Inflation)	**$2,294**

According to these inputs, at age sixty-five your savings will provide $5,397 per month for twenty-five years. This is before taxes. After taxes you will have $4,588 per month. In today's dollars, this is equivalent to $2,294 with a 2.00% annual inflation.

Retirement Income Results for a $7200 Annual Contribution for Twenty-Five Years	
Starting Balance	$0
Annual Contribution	$7,200
Current Age	40
Age of Retirement	65
Years of Retirement	25
Rate of Return Before Retirement	6.00%
Rate of Return During Retirement	6.00%
Current Tax Rate	25.00%
Retirement Tax Rate	15.00%
Expected Rate of Inflation	2.00%
Is This Savings Tax Deferred?	yes
Increase Annual Deposit With Inflation?	no
Total Contributions	**$180,000**
Savings Total Before Taxes	$418,726
Savings Total After Taxes	$355,917
Value Of Savings Today	**$216,942**
Savings Can Provide	
Income Before Taxes	$2,657 per month
Income After Taxes	$2,259 per month
Value of Income in Today' Dollars (With 2.00% Annual Inflation)	**$1,377**

According to these inputs, at age sixty-five your savings will provide $2,657 per month for twenty-five years. This is before taxes. After taxes you will have $2,259 per month. In today's dollars, this is equivalent to $1,377 with a 2.00% annual inflation.

An Ineffective College Savings Approach

Another goal that is commonly ineffective is one recommending a specific savings tool for a child's future college tuition. The question is usually, "How much should I save," or "Which vehicle should I use?" Some may suggest using a Coverdell Education Savings Account (ESA) while others may suggest using a 529 College plan. Moreover, someone may suggest other alternatives. Either way, picking at least one of these investment tools to begin contributing is better than picking none, but each plan has both advantages and disadvantages. Here, though, I will focus on the most talked about vehicles for tax-deferred savings, the ESA and the 529 College plan.

The most notable difference between the ESA and the 529 College plan is the yearly limitations of each. Yet, it amazes me how one can simply recommend a plan without even considering the age of the child, or the type of college institution desired—public or private. If these variables are uncertain, then I would consider saving the most you can in the college savings investment vehicle that allows for the greatest tax-deferrable contributions. Generally, this will most likely be a 529 plan, not the Coverdell ESA.

How We Prevent Wealth

Believe it or not, without trying to consider every variable, or at a minimum, how much time remains until the child reaches his or her college age, one may be eventually disappointed to find later in life that their chosen college plan wasn't the best one, or was simply ineffective. Would a Coverdell ESA, whose current yearly limit of $2,000 per beneficiary, supply enough money over time to cover college expenses if parents begin their child's college saving plan too late? The answer is going to always depend on the different variables that should be considered, but far too often, we do things to set money aside without actually accessing the situation. The parent saving only $2,000 a year for only ten years, may find that $20,000 (or a little greater assuming accumulated interest) may not even cover the entire tuition of a four year state college ten years from now. In fact, if we consider the continually rising cost of public and private universities, $20,000 may definitely be too low an amount. However, some 529 plans, which are state dependent, allows up to a lifetime contribution limit of $300,000 with no yearly contribution limitations, thereby being perhaps the best choice for parents who start saving later in their child's life.

Generally Ineffective Savings Goals

In addition to the few given examples, there are plenty of us who simply save money just for the goal of simply having money. Our savings rates are extremely high, but if asked why we are saving at the rate that we do, we probably wouldn't have the slightest clue other than it simply makes us feel good. Meanwhile, we are not really enjoying life because we can't find a balance between saving and spending. It's not that we don't want to enjoy life, it's because we can actually save too much when we don't have plans in place. We may inhibit our desire to spend on things that would bring fulfillment. How effective is this? Doesn't it make sense to have a purpose or drive behind our savings? Should we really go through life obsessing about spending too much money when we probably don't have to? Saving money should not be a chore; it should be just a systematic way to ensure that future obligations are met.

For several years I was saving money with no defined purpose behind it. I would save for retirement or my son's future college tuition simply because "that's what we are supposed to do." I'd save about $10,000 and have no purpose for it, so the money would eventually end up as a down payment for a car, or for something else such as furniture. And then I would simply start saving money again with no purpose in mind, just in case something came up. In other words, my savings had no drive behind it, rendering it ineffective.

When we save money with no goal in mind, we can easily find that saving money can become boring or cumbersome. As soon as we see something we like, we'll spontaneously and haphazardly find a quick way to spend our saved money just so that it can finally have purpose. After all, the money wasn't being used for anything else, right? When we spend like this, we don't realize how much it sets us back.

Better Goals Defined

So what should we do better once we realize that we have been setting ineffective goals? First, we have to actually *figure out what our goals are.* Second, we have to *understand how to create effective financial goals.* This consists of creating financial goals that are measurable, purposeful, and realistic. Last, we have to *continually evaluate our goals to assess when adjustments are needed,* such as when to begin new goals, stop current goals, or add to our existing goals. By doing so, we minimize our stress of saving too little or too much money. Furthermore, we will realize one of three things: 1) we can realize that we don't have enough money to meet our goals, meaning that we need to somehow increase our earnings; 2) realize that we have just enough money to meet our goals, realizing that we don't have to stress out as much as before; or 3) realize that we save way too much and can be enjoying life by not stressing so much when we spend money on things that we actually want.

To see how creating effective goals works to our benefit, we will use the following examples. A first goal can be to have a home with a $1500 monthly mortgage paid off before we're forty-five years old. This would give us piece of mind because knowing that our home is our biggest expense, when the mortgage payment is gone, we'll have an extra $1500 a month or so in our pocket in retirement. Thus, this goal would work in line with an early retirement goal, because we'll have one less expense to worry about.

A second goal can be to save $50,000, used for a child's future college expenses ten years from now. This amount is based on the *Trends in Higher Education* Website, sponsored by College Board, that shows that the average tuition and fees for the 2010-2011 academic year at a public college is $6224. This amount will mostly likely increase every year.

A third goal can be a desire to have $3,000 of monthly retirement income from the age of sixty to ninety-years-old. Notice that this retirement goal is different than setting an arbitrary retirement percentage.

Last, let's say that we would like to purchase a car with $15,000 cash every five years, assuming that we and our spouse will drive a different model car every ten years or so.

Notice that each of the previous goals was measurable. For instance, we don't want to simply have a home paid in full, we want to have our home *paid off in fifteen years*. We don't simply want to put away money for college, we want to *have $50,000 put away for college in ten years*. Why is it important to make sure our goals are measurable? When we think of our goals, list them, and see what actions need to occur to make them happen, we can begin to see what we actually need to save in order to satisfy each one. Continuing with these examples, we'll see how we would need to satisfy each one.

To have a home paid for in fifteen years, we could either pay extra on a thirty-year mortgage, which many people say that they will do but rarely comply, or finance a home with a fifteen-year mortgage. Because it is less expensive overall to finance a home with a fifteen-year fixed rate mortgage, with respect to interest saved (as will be discussed in chapter 12, We Purchase Thirty Year Mortgages), we'll chose this type of loan. Once this financing takes place, because the term of the loan will be fixed, this goal will be automatically completed, hopefully with no readjustments required.

Our second goal was to have $50,000 put away for a child's tuition ten years from now. For this goal, let's assume that the child is now eight years old, and that we've yet to begin saving for the child's college tuition. In order for us to have $50,000 put away in ten years, not including interest accumulated, we would simply need to put away $416.66 per month. If the child were younger, effectively giving us more time to save, we would have been able to save a smaller monthly amount. However, because we've waited much longer than we probably should have, we'll have to put away the higher amount. Take note that this amounts to more than the annual Coverdell Education Savings Account limit, thereby eliminating it as an option if we are to meet our goal. We would be forced into another investment vehicle such as the 529 College plan or one with greater tax-deferred contribution limits to obtain a $50,000 goal.

The third goal is to have a retirement monthly income of $3,000 from age sixty-five to ninety. For us to figure out how much we need to save to receive $3,000 in monthly retirement income for thirty years, we would have to use as a guideline, an online retirement income calculator, such as Bankrate.com's, *retirement income calculator*, using some assumed variables. Doing so, if we started with a balance of $0 in a tax-deferred account such as a 401(k) or traditional IRA, and assumed an annual return of 6%, a tax rate of 25%, and an inflation rate of 2%, it turns out that we would need to save about $13,000 per year, or $1,083 per month for thirty years, much more than the $600 monthly per the 15% rule if we earned only $4,000 per month.

At this point, if we look at our goals that we have established for ourselves, we'll realize that we must save about $1,499.99 monthly ($416.66 + $1083), not including our mortgage.

The final goal to have $15,000 every five years so that we can purchase a different vehicle is a relatively easy goal to determine. In this case, we would simply assume an initial starting point of $0, and divide $15,000 by sixty months. This calculation does not assume that any interest is accrued with the savings. It yields a monthly required savings amount of $250. So, totaling our required savings amounts of $416.66, $1,083, and $250, we could now see that in order for us to satisfy our goals, we need a total monthly savings of $1,749.66. If we were saving $2,500 a month before, and assuming that the four goals that we used were our only goals that we needed to fulfill to feel comfortable, we have just freed up about $650 monthly for ourselves.

Goal	Time Frame	Savings Needed
Home Paid in Full	Fifteen Years	Refinance to a Fifteen Year Fixed
$50,000 for Child's College	Ten Years	$ 416.66 Monthly
$3000, in Retirement Income from IRA	Thirty Years	$1,083 Monthly
Purchase Another Vehicle	Five Years	$250.00 Monthly
Total Savings Required: $1,749.66 Monthly		

Setting Effective Goals

There is such a thing as saving too much money. If we are miserable because we are stock piling all of our money unnecessarily, instead of doing something fun with it, we may end up kicking the savings habit altogether. The

$650 saved in the previous example can easily be used to buy more things that we desire instead of resisting the temptation to buy them because of a fear that we don't save enough. Or if we still desire to save a total of $2,500 because it makes us feel better, we can easily use the money to accelerate our goals, or add another one such as, save $6,000 a year for travel.

The point of the previous examples was to show that saving towards effective goals is much better than saving blindly. Our goals can easily include getting out of debt on a particular date, saving a certain amount of money for an emergency fund based on a set number of months' worth of living expenses, or saving for a down payment on a first or second home. In either case, we should determine the amount needed to help us reach our goal over a specific time period. With this approach, we can easily add goals as necessary or see where we are falling short in saving for one of our goals once we really evaluate our financial situation.

In the end, when we make our goals effective—measurable, purposeful, and realistic, we can easily balance savings with spending. If our goals do not have such characteristics, we can easily deviate from our current savings by spending our money on something frivolous and less meaningful, thus *preventing wealth.*

Chapter 7

We Get Caught in an Upgrade Cycle

Imagine yourself years ago when you did not have any children, or any responsibilities other than going to school to learn. How great was your life, financially speaking? We lived with our parents and all of our needs were taken care of. Although we may have had a part-time job, all of our money most likely went to us. Maybe some of our money went towards paying for school lunches, buying our own designer clothes or shoes, or even putting gas in the car that was most likely given to us as a hand-me-down from our parents or some other relative. Regardless, all of our money was ours, and we weren't going to give it up to anyone else if we didn't have to. In general, much of it probably went to nothing but unnecessary spending.

Now fast forward to today. Our unnecessary spending did not change; it is now being done in addition to all of our necessary spending. Sometime between when we lived with our parents and now, we added so many other responsibilities to our lives. At some point, we all started spending money, and consequently realized that our standard of living changed. When the job earnings came in, the spending that we were so accustomed to doing when we were living with our parents was somehow different. With our job came the satisfaction of being able to spend our earnings on additional *things*.

As we assessed our pay, we began finding out exactly how much we had to spend on whatever. We could now decide to get married, have children, buy cars, buy a home, pay for soccer practices, or music lessons, or anything else within the constraints of our pay. But, suddenly everyone now had claims to our money. We were okay with this, though, because we were now working, and quite frankly, what else is a job for, right? It's to get the things that we've always wanted but couldn't afford with only a part-time job when we were living with our parents. So we spent and we bought. We at some point decided to bypass the excitement of being able to save or didn't even think about it, and we instead jumped right into the excitement of being able to pay bills.

Let's say that our first job out of college paid us only $1,000 a month, and unrealistically, but for the sake of the following scenarios is money that is exempt from taxes. When we realized that our pay brought home $1,000 a month, we carefully assessed just how much home we could afford and decided that we could pay up to say, $600 a month for an apartment. This was pushing it, but we still had room to spare for the utilities and could still pay about

$100 for our monthly groceries. Maybe we could get by without having a car at that point because we could catch the bus. We were just excited to have finally landed a job. Instead of assessing our monthly income and deciding that we should save $100 a month and rent an apartment that was $500 a month, we did not. We told ourselves that we would instead get the nice pretty apartment now, and that we would save once we earn a little bit more. I mean, we were only making $1,000 a month, right?

After working for the same organization for about a year and getting good evaluations, we miraculously earn a $500 monthly raise. Now our pay has just jumped to $1500 a month. And this pay increase warrants some upgrades, right? Our lease on our apartment comes to an end, so we decide to upgrade to another apartment. Although the apartment is $800 a month, it doesn't matter, because we just received a $500 pay increase. And because we received an increase in pay, we now "just have to buy a car." It may not be a new car, but there is no reason for us to catch the bus to work anymore now that we can afford a car. We graciously walk onto the car lot and after choosing a sufficiently desirable vehicle, we have our seat with the salesman. The salesman asks us the dreaded question, "How much do you want your car payments to be?"

We Get Caught in an Upgrade Cycle

We answer, "Less than $300," because after all, that's about what we have left over from the $500 increase that we recently received. Instead of assessing our monthly income and deciding that we should have saved $100 a month and kept our apartment that was $600 a month, we did not. Or instead of continuing to ride the bus and deciding to keep the $300 in our pocket to save, we did not. We told ourselves that we would get the better apartment now, and get our car now, and that we would save once we earn a little bit more. I mean, we are only making $1,500 a month, right?

A few years go by, and we are now making $3500 a month. We are now making $2,500 more than we did when we first left college. Where do you think we stand now, financially? We have now decided to purchase a home with a $1500 a month mortgage, we have utilities and a cable bill that totals $500 a month, we purchase another car that has a monthly car payment of $500 a month, we got ourselves in a little credit card trouble and are now paying $250 a month in minimum payments; and all the while we are also enjoying our social life, which amounts to spending even more money. At the end of the month, we have nothing remaining. Instead of assessing our monthly income and deciding that we should have saved $100 a month or kept our first apartment where we were paying $600 a month, or bought a house that instead totaled $1,400 a month, we did not. Or instead of continuing to keep the car that we were paying only $300 a month for so that we could keep $200 to save, we did not. We told ourselves that we would get the nice pretty house now, and get our newest car now because we deserved it, and that we would save once we earned a little bit more. I mean, we are only making $3,500 a month, right?

This cycle too often repeats itself. As our pay grows, we add more and more things to what we want, because they all somehow become our "needs." Or we sacrifice our savings, subconsciously, for the things that at the time, we value more. Somehow, we listen to our peers, or those who are worse off than ourselves who convinces us that because we earn a certain amount of money, "we can afford it." All the while, we squeeze ourselves further and further away from being able to save that simple $100 a month.

We consistently tell ourselves that we'll save that $100 once we get another pay raise. But, we do not. At this point, we've already created a mindset that tells us that with every pay raise, we can now afford more things.

We Get Caught in an Upgrade Cycle

Before I purchased my home, I was comfortably paying only $1,000 a month in rent. But then I received a pay raise. And as my income grew, I decided that I could comfortably afford a mortgage as opposed to paying rent—a $500 per month increase. Against my better judgment, it seemed like the right thing to do at the time. Instead of taking the $500 increase and contributing to my IRA or setting the money aside in an emergency fund, I did not. And later when I received another pay increase, I purchased a brand new truck with the money, because "I could afford it" and I was convinced by a friend that the purpose of me working is to get the things that I deserve.

With a brand new home and truck, my savings rate couldn't have changed if I wanted it to, unless I was going to sacrifice by selling something. Although I had an increase in pay of about $1,000 a month, in actuality, my "real" financial status was no different than it was before the pay increase. This is the Upgrade Cycle that I speak of; as our pay goes up, so does our expenses. This is most definitely a way that we *prevent wealth*.

So how do we defeat getting caught up in such a cycle? Is it as easy as saying, "just save the pay raise?" If so, that goal will be ineffective. We have to commit to something. If we don't commit our raises to something, the money will be lost and unaccounted for in the realm of frivolous things. It is up to us, however, to determine what that something will be; this is where setting effective goals comes into play. It is better to set effective goals for our increases as they happen before spending those increases instead of later asking ourselves where it all went. Once we set a specific effective goal for a portion of our pay raise, we should feel comfortable spending the rest. Remember, that we were living quite fine before the increase, so why should we not simply use any raise to work towards our future so that we can help build our wealth? Whatever the case, we must be aware of the Upgrade Cycle, and have it work for us instead of against us.

We Get Caught in an Upgrade Cycle

Chapter 8

We Are Impulse Spenders

There should be no wonder why grocery, toy, department, and other stores are strategically set-up to appeal to the common shopper. Grocery stores strategically place colorful cereal boxes at heights that coincidentally match that of our children. These stores also place candies and other trinkets in the line at the register so that the common shopper can make a last minute purchase. Although a candy bar or lint roller is not necessarily on our shopping list, there's hoping that we give in to our consumerist desires while waiting impatiently in line before cashing-out; it is brilliant marketing.

Merchandise is strategically placed at the front end aisles so that items are prominent and conspicuous. In many cases, before we can even find what we truly want to purchase, such as common staples like milk and bread, we have to pass over many other products and simultaneously restrain ourselves from buying those instead of the staples. We cannot even count the number of times that we go into a grocery store to purchase only milk, but before we leave, we not only have milk but also either cookies, chips, t-shirts, magazines, two liters of soda, or some other item not originally on our list.

We Are Impulse Spenders

From the first minute we step into the store our impulses are involuntarily catered to. If the promotion is good enough to entice us to spend, and if we have a credit card on us and are not disciplined with "good" practices, you better believe that we'll leave the store with impulsively purchased items. This is not a problem for us consumers who are limited in funds at that time, but make no mistake, if the promotion is good enough we will return.

I remember a time during a holiday season when I saw a computer desktop system on clearance for what I remember as an "unbeatable price." It was only $350. It had included a 15" LCD flat-screen monitor and all my computing desires (a 15" LCD monitor was priced at almost $250 individually at that time). I looked it over plenty before I finally told myself that I didn't have the money and therefore was not going to buy it. I hung my head and later left the store without it. But later that night, I reasoned with myself and my spouse that the deal was too good to pass up. I told myself that I would simply use a credit card to purchase the computer (available credit is usually a bad thing for the impulse shopper). Being the non-combative person that she is, she simply obliged. So, she and I ventured out to the store to purchase the computer system.

How We Prevent Wealth

Unfortunately, by the time we returned to the store, the computer was gone. The computers were sold out and none were returning to that store. To my dismay, the clearance item was indeed, cleared. My impulsive need was not satisfied. I had to have it. She and I drove to three other stores that night looking for the "missed opportunity," but we never found that specific system at the promotional price. To this day, I remember my desire; I simply had to have it regardless of whether I "had" the money or not. You can imagine how this may have changed my perspective on passing up great deals. From that moment, I was determined to never let a good deal pass me by. One can see how this kind of experience adds to the mindset of a "wealth preventer."

A few years later, my spouse and I were informed about a wholesale company club that would allow us, the individual consumers, to purchase furniture, appliances, and many other common items at manufacturer's cost. In other words, a sofa that normally sells for $800 in a department store would sell for only $350 at the wholesale company. It was a "great deal" for us, because my spouse and I were soon looking to purchase new furniture anyway. The catch, which we would soon find out, was a high-pressure sales pitch, which without discipline, anyone would buy in to. We were given a tour of the facilities, which included a showing the prices of sample products and the catalogues from which we would soon be able to order. The prices that we were shown were extreme savings relative to the prices of the same products in an average department store. After the tour, we were offered an opportunity to sign up in the club, but the catch was that it was a one-time deal. My adrenaline was at its highest and signing up was a no-brainer, despite the relatively high membership cost of $2500. After all, the cost of savings on furniture would more than pay for the membership. I, with only little hesitation, didn't let this deal pass us up. I had been in this situation before—with the missed opportunity to buy the computer—and I didn't want to revisit the feeling of letting a deal pass me by. So I made the purchase. This time, we at least had the money in a savings account. We became exclusive members to this elite club.

Soon after our membership purchase, we ordered a few items. As promised, the costs were big savings. So far, the impulsive high pressure sale was paying off for both the warehouse club and me. It wasn't until we ordered furniture that we experienced the real cost of the membership.

After tallying our initial costs, we found out that there were additional costs for shipping and handling.

These costs were still insignificant relative to the savings as compared to a retailer. But next we were told that the particular furniture that we had ordered was not a shipping priority because the manufacturer had to first meet the demand of the local retailers. Consequently, it would take a while for the purchases to actually materialize. At this point, it still did not matter to me—what was a few weeks' wait for a savings of $1,000. However, the wait grew longer and longer. I made several calls and left several messages over those weeks. Each time my call was returned, I was told that our furniture was on its way. I was infuriated with what turned out to be an unacceptable wait time. After about twelve weeks of waiting for our furniture, we finally canceled the order. My spouse and I gave up on that particular furniture. My impulse purchase had yet to really pay off.

After a week of kicking myself, and after cooling down, my spouse and I decided to instead visit the local warehouse furniture outlet. Shortly after a look around, we were taken aback. It was here that we noticed that the furniture that we had ordered a few months ago from the wholesaler club was deeply discounted. The total price here was only a few hundred dollars more than what we would have paid at the wholesales' club. So because we had canceled our order from the wholesaler and found a similar deal for the furniture locally, we instead purchased the furniture from the warehouse furniture outlet. It was sickening. We had spent $2,500 for our membership so we could save money on furniture, but up to that point it hadn't been worthwhile. Had we searched locally for our furniture before purchasing the membership, we probably would have saved $2,500 by not having a reason to even visit the wholesaler club; we would have already had furniture. We had now spent money for a membership that we had no immediate plans to use. Furthermore, the anticipated savings on furniture by using our membership had never manifested.

The purchase of our furniture from this furniture outlet made one thing clear; it was not necessary to pay the $2,500 initial membership fee for the club that was supposed to save us so much money, considering that we were only going to make a few furniture purchases anyway. So what I had learned was that instead of jumping on the first "deal" that comes up, I should have practiced some restraint. But clearly, it is hard to do so when our minds are already conditioned to be impulsive spenders. Still, I was determined to use my membership until I purchased enough items that would at a minimum amount to $2,500.

How We Prevent Wealth

Almost a year later, we tried our luck again at the wholesale club when we were surprisingly looking for some additional furniture. This time we actually received the furniture that we ordered. Although it was a real pain to get the furniture delivered, we finally made a successful purchase, almost making our membership worth its price. But after this purchase, it turned out that we still had more to buy until we could accumulate a total savings of $2,500. To this day, the savings still have not added up to the original membership cost. And because I am still determined to break even, five years later, I'm still paying an annual membership renewal fee of $100; I'd hate to have spent $2,500 but never break even. So instead of ending the membership, I have trapped myself into paying the $100 annual renewal fee in hopes that I will one day purchase enough items to make the membership worth it.

This story of my impulsive purchase is only one of what many of us do every day. My "had-to-have it" mentality has cost me plenty. Instead of truly assessing how much of a deal the membership really was, I purchased it and figured it out later.

Our Impulsive Habits

We make impulsive purchases on a small scale every time that we visit stores without a shopping list. Instead of a high-pressure sales tactic by a wholesale club representative, we are bombarded with bright neon sale signs, or clearance racks, or "roll-back" notices. Every time that we turn on the television, advertisers are showing us what's new or what things we just have to have. When we open up magazines we are met with the aroma of fragrances and the endorsements of products by celebrities. When we open up our Web browsers to visit Web sites, we are often so bombarded with advertisements that we can't even find the content that actually belongs to the site. We are subconsciously pressured to go and take a look at what's new and what's such a great deal. And we spend. And we do it repeatedly. And we do so often. And like my $2,500 membership, in the end, we find out that we probably don't really need what we purchase.

We constantly give in to our impulsive desires, and if not our impulsive desires, or own curiosity. We don't realize how quickly our spending adds up, and before we know it, our weekly pay has been exhausted. We begin taking money from our savings accounts or using credit cards to extend our income. As we continue to spend more of our savings or accumulate more debt to buy more things, we get further and further away from building wealth.

Quite frankly, in an innovating world that is creating new technologies and conveniences coupled with strategic marketing, it is difficult to curb our spending. But in the end, we must apply will power—at least until we are comfortably saving for retirement and meeting our effectively set financial goals. Every dollar that we spend on something frivolous is a dollar that we use to prevent our wealth. We claim that we don't have extra money to save, but it's because we are too busy buying things with our "extra" money.

The point should be clear—we almost always have money to save. Yet, we make the unconscious decision to spend impulsively on things that are not needed instead. This is clearly a barrier to building wealth. Once again, we prevent ourselves from having a comfortable future. We keep ourselves working way into our golden years. We *prevent wealth.*

Ultimately, we have to understand that buying things, be it impulsively purchased or not, will always take away from some other purchase. Every dollar that is spent frivolously on gum in the checkout line, or every fifty dollars spent on an outfit simply because it was on sale, is money that is taken away from spending on something that we may really want or money that could have otherwise been saved, which would help us accumulate wealth. The only way to scale back our impulsive spending is to understand the difference between a "want" and a "really want." We can minimize going to stores, but that may be unreasonable for many people.

Determining "Wants" vs. "Really Wants"

I'm reminded of a visit to a local electronics retailer, and like the stereotypical male, I reveled in all of the retailer's goodness. I walked eloquently through each aisle looking at each product. I imagined where each of them would fit in my home.

I checked out the televisions, the audio receivers, the game systems, and even the refrigerators with built in television monitors. I looked at the tablets, mp3 players, movies, computers, and much more. I was amazed at how many things that I truly wanted. And through this entire window shopping experience, I hadn't even made it to car stereos—the reason I was there in the first place.

Of course with every product that I picked up, I analyzed if I really *needed* it. And that is when I realized that we rarely *need* anything. In most cases, economic decisions really come down to wants vs. really wants. In other words, because our money is scarce (there is a limited supply) we have to choose between spending money on, say, a tablet or an mp3 player, because in many cases we only have enough money for one or the other. And if we do have the money for both, well, then we may not have the extra money left over for something else, say a computer.

I realized that none of the items I looked at were *needs*, but just wants. So it stands that we need to strategically spend our money so that we purchase the really wants vs. wants. How does one know which is which? How does this help protect us against making impulsive buys?

The *really wants* are those things that will bring us the greatest value. If we can reason ourselves out of a decision because we would much rather have something different, then what we are looking at is most likely just a want. For example, a tablet that I was looking at was awesome, but then I begin asking myself how much more can it really do that my laptop couldn't? Not much, I determined, so the tablet became just a want. My car stereo in my new, used car, had only a tape deck and no auxiliary or USB inputs for a music player, but I *really wanted* to listen to my own personal selection of music in my car. So I determined that the car stereo was my *really want.*

We have to understand that the money that we have can only purchase a limited number of things. And we then have to convert those things into priorities based on "wants" and "really wants." Had I adopted this attitude before spending $2500 on my club membership, I would have probably realized that all I *really wanted* was a great deal on some furniture at the time, not great deals on furniture for life. We have to learn to protect the money we have, so that we can maximize the amount we can use to build wealth.

Chapter 9

We Are Slaves to our Credit Cards

Throughout college and thereafter, up into about three years after I had started working, I was paying off credit card debts. It was not because I was using credit cards to survive (i.e. paying the monthly utilities, buying groceries, or paying for clothes) until I landed my next job, it was because I purchased "wants" for the family. I had intentions of paying later, but miserably failed in doing so. I had an electronics store credit card that was used to purchase a 43" television, a game system, and some other stuff that I couldn't remember if asked. I had store credit from a carpet store that was used to purchase carpet for a tiny apartment, because my son "needed" it to comfort his knees when he began crawling. And I had two other bank cards that I *think* were used to buy furniture. I still have the financial spreadsheet on my computer to show these balances and the three years that it took me to pay them off. In these three years of paying down debts, I was definitely a slave to my credit card.

How Do We Become Slaves?

When we purchase things with our credit cards, only to have to pay minimum payments later, we start a vicious cycle. A $20 monthly minimum payment will seem small in comparison to the $1,000 that we just spent, and it will be seen as an easily manageable expense, until we continue our cycle of spending.

Although maybe not immediately after we max out our first card, we will eventually decide that we "need" something else. And just because it's our lucky day, we'll easily find that the something else we "need" to purchase can be purchased with a credit plan that boasts "no payments due for six months and 0% financing for eighteen months." This time, however, the something else would be more expensive, such as some furniture, a television set, or some other contraption that cost upward of $5,000. But, we'll tell ourselves that we are still okay, because when the minimum payments start, they too are relatively low. As we repeat this cycle, we'll eventually find that we have maxed out our available credit.

When we realize that we are no longer eligible for new credit is just about the same time that our "promotional" offers will just so happen to end. And because we were paying minimum payments all the while, our card balances will not be too far off from where they began. This is when the real trouble starts—when we become slaves. The interest rates that were deferred because of the promotions will set in. Despite our best efforts, the balances of the cards won't decrease because of our minimum payments, and even if they do, this is when the true emergency sets in. Because we have consistently relied on our credit cards instead of having the extra money to make purchases, the balances increase again. And the cycle repeats.

We will try and try unsuccessfully to lower the balances of our credit cards, but because we also have other financial obligations, we'll find that we are only able to pay our minimum balances. We'll find out the effect of how interest rates affects our balances, and we'll also feel the effect that it will have on our lives—we'll feel like we are in servitude to our debts. We'll feel that there is nothing that we can do. And we'll have no other choice than to put off saving for other things, so we can pay down debts. Short of ruining our credit score, we will not be able to escape these payments. Our credit cards will have control over us, and there will be nothing that we can do about it. Thus, we'll have no other choice than to *prevent wealth* by making huge interest payments on things that was purchased in a distant past.

How Long Will We be in Servitude?

What if we had the following credit cards? (The minimum payments are assumed to be 2% of the balance.)

- Credit Card 1
    - Balance - $5,000.00
    - Annual Interest - 18%
    - Minimum Payment - $100.00
- Credit Card 2
    - Balance - $2,500
    - Annual Interest - 22%
    - Minimum Payment - $50.00
- Credit Card 3
    - Balance - $1,000
    - Annual Interest - 12%
    - Minimum Payment - $20.00

If we were to try to pay down these debts, assuming that we no longer charge a single penny to these cards, it will take years to be rid of these credit card balances. According to credit card calculator, we would be stuck with the following if we made only the minimum payments:

Credit Card 1: It will take us 472 months to be rid of our debt, and in this time we would pay $13,396.73 in interest.

Credit Card 2: It will take us 859 months to be rid of our debt, and in this time we would pay $20,551.93 in interest.

Credit Card 3: It will take us 99 months to be rid of our debt, and in that time we would pay $544.95 in interest.

So yes, it would take us almost *72 years* to be rid of all of our debt with over *$34,000 in interest payments made*! What if we added these bills to the student loans that we took out and discussed in Chapter 5, *We Don't Educate Ourselves*? We would now have accumulated lifetime interest payments of $49,085.61 on a total debt of $59,000.

This $49,000 could be used for retirement contributions, investing in a business, or anything more productive than simply paying it as interest to the financial institution of whom we owe. Perhaps it could be used to take a course in investing, or saving for a payment on a home. It could instead be used to contribute to anything that has the ability to help us accumulate wealth.

To Use, or Not to Use Credit Cards

After financially accomplishing the feat to pay off my credit cards, I still struggled with credit cards for years. Not in the sense of running their balances up until they were maxed out, or in a way where I had too many credit cards, but in the sense of determining whether credit cards were "bad" or "good."

On the one hand, some say that credit cards are bad and that there is no need for them—at all. And there have even been books written that denounce the use of credit cards: "Oh what bad practices their companies have! Their companies will post your payments late! They will hike up your interest rates! They will not give you your "reward" points!" So for a short while, I took this as my own belief.

On the other hand, according to teachings from actual certified personal finance advisers who use text book explanations, credit cards are great: "They help build credit. They provide "reward" incentives. They afford you with personal protections that are not available if using a debit card." So for a short while, I also took this as my own belief.

Luckily, like all things in the media, we should always listen to both sides of every argument or story so that we can formulate our own opinions. While there are many advantages to using credit cards, the advantages do not come without risk. Some of the risks are:

- Impulsively spending more on items that we can't afford
- Paying more for items that we impulsively purchased if we have to start making interest payments
- Having one more thing that allows our personal identities to be stolen
- Damaging our credit ratings if we miss or make late payments
- In some cases, paying fees on inactive cards or being assessed expensive cash withdrawal fees that accrue interest beginning at the time of withdrawal
- Having a high debt to income, when balances are carried, which may lead to higher interest rates on loans than if no balance were carried
- Having too many cards with too much available credit, which is considered a negative factor by lenders

Knowing that all of these risks exist, why are we so liberal when using credit cards? Why do so many people carry so many credit cards? Are multiple credit cards being used to "enjoy" the perks such as frequent flyer miles, hotel stays, zero percentage financing, and so forth, or are they being used to artificially expand our income? If the former is the case, we should ask ourselves how often are our perks redeemed, and if our answer is not often, we should next ask ourselves whether the possession of multiple cards is really worth all of the risks described. If the latter is the case, we should simply get rid of our cards now before we find ourselves in far more debt than we can handle. The following are my established guidelines for credit cards:

Credit cards *should not* be used as our primary emergency fund. As long as we believe and rely on credit to be available through an emergency, we have no real incentive to save and fund an emergency with cash. If we don't have cash standing by now, what makes us think that we'll have the cash to pay off a new and unanticipated credit card bill if we have to make an emergency purchase? If we don't have cash on hand, the cost of our emergencies may very well increase because of unanticipated and drawn out payments that could possibly accrue interest. We may also be subjected to late payment fees if we find ourselves in such a situation.

We should instead, request an additional checking account with our bank. Every month, we should transfer an amount of cash to it—$20, $50, $100, whatever, for a set number of months—up until we reach an emergency account goal that equals the balance of the credit card that we are relying on. After reaching this goal, we should no longer carry the credit card with us to keep ourselves out of trouble. Later, when we get in a bind, we'll be able to use the debit card that's linked to the checking account that we've established for our emergency purpose.

Credit cards *should not* be our financial cushion to hold us to the end of the week, month, or through a holiday. The same unanticipated costs that may occur by using a credit card for an emergency are the same when we use a credit card for the sole purpose of "getting by." If we don't have the money to pay for something *now*, then we don't have the money to pay for it later. This buy-it-now, pay-for-it-later type attitude is a perpetually impending financial downfall for many of us, to say the least, being the beginning of a debt accumulation cycle for so many of us.

We should strive to always have monies set aside that will account for unanticipated events such as an unplanned bill, an unexpected flight, or a renter who unexpectedly moves out of our investment property. We can't always rely on stability in our jobs, but we should be able to rely on money that we set aside for specific troubles so that we don't have to use credit cards for a financial cushion. For example, the income that we thought we'd have after a holiday season might not necessarily be available if our hours are reduced or if we are laid off.

If we don't have the liquid cash to immediately pay off our credit cards after making a purchase, forcing us into a position where we will have to pay interest charges, then we shouldn't buy things on credit. If we choose to do this at any time, then we are simply "getting by." Instead of "getting by," by using credit, we should concentrate on how we can earn more money so that we can get out of such a cycle. Do we have the means to increase our income, sell things (even if it's our nice, new, pretty car), or cut spending? Unfortunately, we rarely do these things.

The easiest way to prevent the "getting by" cycle is to simply cut back on spending. For example, if we routinely spend an extra $100 a month using a credit card, we can instead easily stop this by cutting out a monthly payment that yields an extra $100 per month. Do we *need* a smart phone that locks us into an expensive data plan? Do we *need* super-high-speed Internet or can we rely on just high-speed Internet?

Credit cards *should* be cautiously used to reap the benefits of reward points, air miles, or cash back. To get many of the perks that credit card companies offer, we have to spend *lots* of money that we would probably not spend otherwise. For example, with a travel rewards card that my bank issues, one has to spend $30,000 just to collect 30,000 points, which would reward the recipient with only a $600 round-trip air ticket. Or, although a gas card may promise 5% cash-back for qualified gas purchases, we would have to spend $3,000 a year to receive $150, or less obviously, $12.50 per month. In the end, is spending $30,000 just to get $600 really worth it? Is receiving $12.50 a month really worth the extra administrative tracking and increased risks if we are paying that same amount in monthly interest?

In many cases, one credit card can be used to reap the benefits of these perks. However, we have to understand that most reward cards carry higher interest rates than non-rewards cards, and some even have annual fees. For example, an airline may offer a free round-trip ticket for signing up for their credit card, but in most cases an annual fee of $75 or more will be immediately applied, and the interest rate on purchases made with the card will most likely be over 15%. So if we get caught up in some bad months where we can only afford minimum payments for whatever reason our reward perks may quickly lose their value.

Credit Cards can often be carefully used to protect us or our businesses from fraud or questionable transactions. They can also be used when traveling and for other conveniences when we already have the cash in another account to cover our transactions. When we know that we will pay our payments on time, such that we pay no interest on our purchases, a credit card can offer convenient protections.

In terms of fraud, credit cards offer certain protections under the Fair Credit Billing Act (FCBA) that protects us differently than debit cards that are linked to checking accounts, which are governed by the Electronic Fund Transfer Act (EFTA). For example, the maximum liability that we pay for unauthorized use of a credit card is $50 when the fraud is discovered. But with a debit card, not only will our cash be taken from our accounts if we don't discover the unauthorized use and report it within sixty days, depending on the type of unauthorized use, there can also be unlimited liability, meaning we may never see the money again. Some banks, through certain programs, do offer a zero liability program, in which the consumer is not liable for transactions performed by unauthorized users, but these protections are not law.

In terms of questionable transactions, we should strive never to provide our debit card information to a company when purchasing things over the phone or on an unsecured website. We have no way of knowing how and where the information will be recorded by the company. What are the company's practices? What happens if we discover that the company "made a mistake" and charged too much? If we were using a debit card linked to our spending account, this money would be gone until a dispute is brought between our banks and the company. Who is right—the company or the consumer?

If we have the money to pay cash for traveling and were going to purchase, say, an airline ticket or a rental vehicle anyway, then in this case, *if* our credit card company pays for some sort of insurance, then we can use our credit card to take advantage of these protections. For example, most credit cards provide auto accident insurance for rental cars (which saves up to $30 per day when not purchased through the rental company), and extensive travel accident insurance for flights (providing up to $1,000,000 to the card holder's beneficiaries in the event of a plane crash). Credit cards can be used to maximize our protections if we are careful not to pay interest, and if know that we have monies immediately available to pay our balances in full.

Alternatives to Credit Cards:

In the end, though, do we even need credit cards? They may have their conveniences, but they are not necessarily needed. Financial Institutions can come up with all sorts of reasons why we actually need credit cards, and we probably can too. But in actuality, the answer is, "we don't." We don't *need* a separate credit card for online protections if we have a debit card linked to a separate checking account that has its own amount of funds in it that are used extensively for online purchases or over-the-phone transactions. As long as we check the card's account balance every couple days, we should be able to catch most fraud before it grows out of hand. If fraud does occur, and if we have dedicated funds in a separate account, we should be able to wait for a claim to be processed because our "real" money is never touched. It is so unfortunate that we have established an ideology that suggests that we need a credit card.

Options to Build Credit without Credit Cards

Fixed Rate Loans:

The most suggested reason for actually *needing* a credit card is to "build credit," but the fact is, we don't. I'm not suggesting that establishing credit is not important, but what I am suggesting is that there are many alternatives to credit cards that help us to establish credit. In fact, there are many financial debts that we may ultimately accrue in the beginning of a career that will help us establish our credit. We may take on a reasonable amount of student loans, or even borrow a small loan for a first vehicle, both of which "builds credit." And unlike payments on a credit card, the payments on student loans and vehicles are fixed. Meaning, once we run out of credit, it has served its purpose, and there's no more available to get out of hand with. Am I saying that we should all get loans instead of credit cards? No, but my point is why is having a credit card necessary to "build credit" if we are already doing it in alternative ways?

We, however, do not market or heavily advertise these alternatives to building credit, because too many of us say that we *need* credit cards.

The Secured Credit Card:

Another alternative to "building credit," but without using an actual "credit card" is a secured credit card. A secured credit card is one that is "secured" by money that we have, and is transferred to a card that has a credit card merchant's logo on it, which can be used for credit card transactions. These are usually used for first time credit builders or for people with bad credit who are trying to reestablish credit. Either way, it is an alternative to an actual credit card. We have the ability to spend and use as a credit transaction, up to an amount that we set. Secured credit cards are easily obtainable. We just have to make sure that the one that we receive has no or low fees, and that it reports to the credit bureaus.

Conveniently enough for financial institutions, we still choose to have credit cards. We are even provided incentives to have them. At college campuses, students are offered anything from key chains to t-shirts just to sign up for credit cards. At department stores we are offered 0%

financing for up to twenty-four months. Our banking institutions offer us rewards points, or travel miles. Unfortunately for all of us, there are far more *perceived* conveniences of having a credit card, than there are reasons to not have a credit card. But what we don't understand is that by using them, if we are not in control, we may ultimately prevent wealth. So, if we are going to have and use credit cards, we have to be careful to never pay interest to the institutional owner of our credit cards. Money going towards interest is money that can easily be applied to establishing another effective financial goal.

The "Unfortunate Wealth Preventers"

Contrary to popular belief, banks are not run by morons. Their systems are setup so that they make a profit. And along with the interest that they collect off of mortgages, they also collect interest off of other loans and credit cards. Although we try to "game" the system by taking advantage of "free" plane tickets or other trinkets, nothing is free in actuality. If we are incentivized to spend money to receive points or miles, then even if we never pay interest on the card, we may make a few purchases on our credit cards just to receive rewards. So although some of us may succeed in "cheating" the banks, you better believe that some of us will eventually get caught up in trying to game the systems; we will call them the "unfortunate wealth preventers." And this is where many of us have fallen. Once we buy into the hype that we actually need a credit card, and then begin using it as an extension of our income, we become hooked. Before we know it, we feel trapped and helplessly riddled in debt. In combination with our impulsive habits, we end up in a bad position.

Why pay the banks when we can pay ourselves? As was just shown, there are several alternatives to credit cards. Ultimately, though, we have to choose whether or not we want to take on the risks of using credit cards. We have to know ourselves. If we have a history of making bad financial decisions with respect to credit card usage, we may not need to have a credit card. We have to determine how much financial control we actually want.

We have to ask ourselves our reasons for having a credit card. If our reasons are for an emergency use, or to have as a financial buffer, then we may soon find ourselves headed in the wrong financial direction. As previously emphasized, credit cards does provide conveniences. However, if we find ourselves paying interest on the purchases made with our card, we can, and often do end up in financial trouble. Thus, we end up *preventing wealth*.

Only we know ourselves. If we have yet to learn financial discipline, we should not use credit cards—avoid becoming a slave to them.

We Are Slaves to Our Credit Cards

Chapter 10

We Change Our Cars Too Often

Over the last thirteen years, I had over ten vehicles and all for different reasons. My first vehicle was a $2,500, five-year-old, 1994 Mercury Cougar. A little more than a year later, I upgraded my Cougar to a 1998 Mercury Mountaineer that had cost $16,500. Three years later, the Mountaineer was totaled in a rain storm.

After receiving a cash payout from my insurance company, for the totaled loss of the Mountaineer, I took the cash from and purchased a 1994 Honda Accord for about $4,500. After about a year, I was shuffling around cars between my spouse and me, and had given the Accord to her. When I gave her the Accord, I purchased a 2001 Chrysler Concord from the Summerville Auto Auction in South Carolina, where I had paid only $2,500. I drove the Concord for a little more than a year, up until the engine failed. After that, I told myself that I was done with older cars and decided to finance a 2006 Ford F-150 for about $22,000.

Up until this point, the only car that I had financed was the Mountaineer. But, after realizing that I didn't quite like the model F-150 that I had purchased on top of not wanting to make monthly payments, I sold it for $16,500 and purchased another Honda Accord for $5500 cash, to once again try to save money. This worked out well for about a year. I kept the Honda Accord until I bought another vehicle—a Ford F-150 once again—that I financed for $36,000 because just like the Upgrade Cycle predicted, I had received a huge pay increase, but quickly allocated the extra money to a new monthly note. It wasn't until recently that I realized what a moron I was. These are just the vehicles that *I* have owned.

When my spouse and I had first started dating in 2000, she had a 1997 Mazda 626. Later in 2000 she upgraded to a 1998 Acura Integra. After about two years of having the Integra, and now as a married couple, we upgraded her vehicle to a full-sized, almost brand-new 2003 Honda Accord; it was the dealership's demonstration model. Three years later, when I realized that I didn't want to make car payments anymore, because we were "stretching our paycheck too thin," I sold the Accord and downgraded to a more stylish, but used, 2001 Honda Accord.

Eventually, I felt pretty bad that we had to sell her 2003 Honda Accord. So, when I purchased my Honda Accord, after the first Ford F-150 I had financed, I traded in her 2001 Accord to lease her 2008 Acura TSX. I paid the

2008 Acura TSX off in full in a little under three years, but just as I had realized after my 2009 F-150 purchase, I was a moron. Although we had a nice pretty paid off, luxury vehicle, I realized a few months later that we were car rich and cash poor; we had little money in the bank because our $22,000 cash had just paid off a vehicle. I later sold the TSX in 2010, downgrading and paying $8,900 cash for a 2001 Honda Accord. In that same year, I sold my 2009 F-150, downgrading and paying $2,750 cash for a 1997 Honda Civic.

There is no secret that I've wasted plenty of money by purchasing so many vehicles over the past thirteen years, and the prices above don't even include the various taxes, insurance, registration, and other fees. This has no doubt cut into my future financial well-being, and has definitely prevented me from building wealth. Although some cars were paid in full using cash, and others were paid in full quickly before their loans matured, in the end, it still was plenty of money wasted—money that could have been in my pocket had I purchased and stuck with just our original vehicles.

My story is not uncommon. Purchasing many cars, because we focus merely on a car's aesthetics instead of its utility, is a sure way that we prevent wealth. Needless to say, I have hopefully learned my lesson, and have vowed only to purchase another car when all of my financial goals to secure my future are being met.

The Rapidly Decreasing "Asset"

To make matters financially worse, not only are we wasting money when we purchase multiple vehicles, we're wasting money purchasing "assets" that rapidly lose their values. For whatever reason, like the justification for every other poor financial decision we make, we swear that we are making the right decision. When we purchase our cars brand new, we exacerbate the situation. Although we could save thousands by purchasing a slightly older but similar model, we pay the excessive prices. We tell ourselves that it's okay, and justify our purchase by claiming that we'll drive our cars until the wheels fall off. Some of us do, but many of us do not.

For proof of excessive depreciations, we need to look no further than the trade-in or private retail prices recommended for our vehicles as listed on popular and informative Web sites such as Kelly Blue Book, Edmunds, or NADA; new cars may lose their values rather quickly. For example, in 2011, the 2008 TSX that I financed for about $30,000 had a suggested retail value of only $21,635 according to Kbb.com; the trade-in value, assuming the car is in excellent condition, was only $17,575. There are two main ways we can interpret these numbers. One, our car would lose at least 41% of its value if we were to trade it in to get another, or two, we could purchase this car used with low mileage for a bargain of 27% off of the original value. Yet, we rarely see slightly used cars as bargains. We don't want hand-me-downs, we say. We get tunnel vision and the mind-set that new is always better. Although the new and older models can have similar, if not the exact same features, we purchase the newest models. In fact, with the exception of subtle differences, the 2004 TSX is very similar to the 2008 TSX when comparing style and features.

We spend thousands of dollars on cars that we inevitably will exchange every four or five years. If we know that we are going to do this, why can't we minimize the amount of money that we spend when possible by purchasing slightly used vehicles? Even reliability and safety as an answer should not be a strong case for a new vehicle if those are the only reasons; extended warranties that cover almost all of the vehicle's parts and labor can usually be purchased from the manufacturer for less than $1,500, which when added to a used car price is still thousands of dollars in savings. Imagine if we were to research and purchase a desirable car for just half the average selling price of vehicles, and did this every five years. We would save so much money over time.

Purchasing Too Much Vehicle

Many of us really can't afford the vehicles we buy. It is not uncommon to see people who earn no more than $40,000 annually, driving a car with a price that is even higher than their annual income. We've been conditioned to look at the monthly payments of a vehicle, not the overall price. And the dealerships know this, so they make sure they exploit it. When we visit car dealerships, the first question that we are usually asked is, "what do you want your monthly payments to be?" As long as we can get financing for the amount that we say, if we can meet their credit criteria, we will walk out of the dealership with a car. The vehicle will simply be financed to meet our needs; when the dealership or bank tells us that we are approved, we are often so excited about the approval that we don't even pay attention enough to learn the true total cost of the vehicle; the price that is on our Truth in Lending statement.

To help us prevent wealth, the banking institutions allow us to extend our loan terms, in many cases, so that we can afford our cars with "reasonable" payments. There was a time when thirty-six months was a reasonable loan term, and then it increased to forty-eight months. More and more, we are seeing vehicles that are routinely financed for seventy-two or eighty-four months—seven years! And we are ignorant to the fact that it is only these extended loan terms that make our payments affordable and "reasonable."

Even still, while these are indeed issues, the biggest problems come after we decide that we no longer want the vehicle for whatever reason; we decide that we want to trade the vehicle for another one, or it gets totaled and leaves us with a remaining balance. When we purchase a car with eighty-four month financing, we will undoubtedly be offered the highest possible interest rate; as the loan is extended further out, we become more of a risk to the lending institution. This, coupled with the rapidly depreciating value of cars, becomes a financial nightmare. When we decide to trade a car in, we are shocked to find that we owe much more for the vehicle than its actual value.

Being Upside Down

I knew someone who held an interest rate of 18% on a $20,000 vehicle under a five year term. In this person's case, the vehicle was unfortunately totaled in an accident after only making eighteen monthly loan payments. Although this individual had auto insurance, the insurance company could only pay the suggested retail value. As we learned, this value may rapidly change. Due to the rapid depreciation of the totaled vehicle, it was only valued at $14,000. At 18% interest, on a $20,000 loan for sixty months, even after paying on the car for eighteen months, the amount owed was roughly $15,469. This of course left $1,469, including the deductible that the owner had to pay before the insurance company covered their portion of the claim. This could have all been avoided had the individual purchased a less expensive car and understood that he should have shopped around for a lower interest rate, or reduced their loan terms; but according to the individual, the terms were reasonable because of the low monthly payments.

In the previous case, suppose after eighteen months the vehicle wasn't totaled but the owner decided to trade it in for an "upgrade." In my experience, the dealer will most likely offer a value that would be even lower than what's presented as a trade-in value as given by Kelly Blue Book, Edmunds, or other appraiser companies. In fact, I was once told by a sales manager that he hated these appraiser companies, because the appraiser companies "weren't the ones buying the cars." That pretty much told me that our cars are worth what the dealership says that they are worth, which maximizes the dealership's profits.

So, to go forth with our "upgrade" we'll assume that because we are trading the vehicle in at the eighteen month point, the dealership is generous and "gives" us a trade-in value of $12,500. In this case, the trade-in would be "upside-down" in value; so now, the $2969 ($15,469 - $12,500) has to be added into or rolled on to any new financing, if we aren't prepared to pay it off separately. If we upgrade to another $20,000 vehicle, now we would be paying $20,000 plus the $2969 in "negative equity" for our next car, not including taxes and fees.

If down the line, say thirty-two months into the new loan, we once again decide to upgrade, or if our car is totaled, we will find ourselves upside down even more, and would have to simply roll a bigger chunk into the newest loan. What if this situation were the same for a couple who wanted to upgrade both their cars at the same time? Many of us find ourselves in these situations, and quite frankly, the only way to remedy this is to keep the cars that we are upside-down in until we are ready to pay cash for another.

The Automobile Lease

Another great example of the "too many cars" theory is the lease. While a lease may have smaller payments over a shorter time period than financing the latest model vehicle in full, it simply doesn't dawn on us that at the end of the lease we will no longer have a car unless we decide to refinance the vehicle as a purchase, or roll into a new lease. We can have three nice new cars for the next nine years, assuming only thirty-six month leases, but even after paying on three different cars for nine years, we still wouldn't own a car. How can we possibly save as much as we need in an emergency or retirement account if we, for the next nine years, decide to continually lease three different vehicles at the average cost of $400 per month? Additionally, most lease financing companies require insurance premiums on their leased vehicles that are much more inclusive, and therefore more expensive, than premiums for financed vehicles. After leasing a car for nine years, paying $400 monthly, we would end up paying over $43,000 and still not own a vehicle.

New Cars or Leases Are Not the Enemy

To be clear, if we want new and nice model vehicles, there should be no reason why we can't purchase

them *if* all of our sound financial goals are being meet, and
we have saved enough money to keep our loan terms and
rates as low as possible. The problem is not necessarily the
new car, though, but it is the fact that we prevent wealth by
not focusing on the potential savings of shorter terms and
lower rates, or we put our savings secondary to our new
cars.

If we have succeeded in building an emergency
fund, are saving for a set retirement income, and have
savings set aside for our children's college or other
effective goals, then we should buy a car that we want,
within reason, if that is something that we truly value.
However, our problem is that our goals are not usually
being met and our capacity for reasoning what constitutes a
reasonable car is usually skewed by marketing and a desire
to impress other people.

If we have not set a goal to determine how much we
need to save for retirement, are heavily in debt with student
loans, have huge balances on our credit cards, or have any
other obligations that prevent us from building wealth such
that we can't have financial freedom in our golden years,
we need to not purchase expensive vehicles or if possible,
not finance a car at all. Money that goes towards the
payment of high-priced vehicles is money that is not

applied to minimize bills and maximize savings. Imagine if we didn't have a $400 payment on a vehicle. The money could easily go towards building an emergency account if that has yet to be established, contributing to an eligible retirement account, or adding more to our short or long term financial goals.

A Reasonable Car That Does Not Prevent Wealth

A reasonable car is the least expensive car that can reliably and practically get us from point A to B. Our reliable and practical car should be very conservative; it should do everything that we need it to do, not necessarily everything we want it to do. It shouldn't matter whether we make $25,000 or $250,000 annual; we should use any extra money beyond the purchase of a reliable car to reduce our debts and set effective goals. A reliable car is easily researched using *Consumer Reports*, online car forums, or periodic articles from online sources such as *Yahoo!*, *Edmunds*, or *KBB*.

The reasonable car that I purchased is fourteen years old. I currently only have a mortgage debt, but because I am trying to save money to refinance my home that has rapidly depreciated, I will not spend any money to buy beyond my reliable car; I paid only $2750—cash—for my car, and it gets me from home to work with no problem. I have a vehicle that is reliable, and will be kept until I am totally back on track, meaning until I have refinanced my home into a fifteen-year mortgage, or sold it, as well as having my effective goals well established.

Clearly, many of us cannot afford to purchase a car with cash, but want a very reliable vehicle. We simply have to be responsible enough to keep in mind what our end goals are—to minimize, or avoid if at all possible, preventing wealth. Generally speaking, auto loans should never extend beyond thirty-six months. Any terms greater than thirty six months usually carry higher interest rates, and are more prone to leaving the buying with negative equity.

The main point of these few examples is for us to understand that we can't continue to go overboard when purchasing vehicles. It shouldn't matter how "reasonable" a financing company can make our car payments. When financing a car, we have to pay close attention to the total amount we are paying, including taxes, warranties, registration, and interest. And we need to minimize the length of our loans, while striving to never finance a car for more than thirty-six months. Ultimately, we need to learn how to pay our cars off and keep them, at least until we can pay cash for the next one, or have well established effective goals in place.

We've purchased way too many vehicles, and have wasted plenty of money doing so. We have to really think about our car payments and purchases that set us back. We have to reevaluate these purchases and choose not to prevent our wealth.

Chapter 11

We Think Renting Is Throwing Away Money

Think of how many times we've heard, "You're just throwing your money away if you rent" or similarly, "You're just making someone else rich by paying *their* mortgage." This phrase has swept America for years with regard to home ownership. "It's the American Dream," we praise. Recently, in what has been dubbed the subprime mortgage crisis, it has been the downfall for many Americans. There are various reasons to postulate as to why too many Americans have and continue to lose their homes, but perhaps focusing on other phrases commonly heard can give us a little insight into just one of several theories.

Contrary to popular belief, it is perfectly okay to not own a home—and there are many reasons why this is true. But then it is argued, "A home is an investment!" Fortunately for us, the English dictionary gives us several definitions of what an investment is. Let's go with an investment being, "an act of devoting time, effort, or energy to a particular undertaking with the *expectation* of a worthwhile result." If this is the definition that people speak of when describing a home as an investment, then we should all be obliged to agree. We may very well end up devoting plenty of time and money into a home that can potentially be nothing but a giant headache—something that is never worth the "investment."

When I moved to Georgia, I continually went back and forth on the decision to purchase or rent a home. I was toying with the thought that if I did purchase a home, it would most likely turn into a rental property as I expected to live in Georgia for only a few years. So, with that in mind, I initially decided to rent. I found a nice home in a nice suburban area that I'd began renting for only $1,000 monthly. At this point, the only extra "mandatory" payments were of course, rental insurance and the normal utilities—water and electricity--which came to no more than $400, on average. So, I had a nice home that I was renting for less than $1,500. I didn't have to worry about any extra expenses or fees, and I could leave at any time without a financial penalty, assuming that my lease agreement had been fulfilled. And, even if the lease agreement wasn't fulfilled, all I would have to do is pay a month's rent as penalty and lose my security deposit—only about $2,000 in all. A steep price, but after paying it, I would have the flexibility to leave, without it adversely affecting my credit score. The roughly $1,500 per month in total was a pretty good deal, all things considered. Had I chosen to live in and rent an apartment, I could have paid even less, and would still have the flexibility to leave on demand.

After about a year, it turned out that I really enjoyed the area. I liked the area so much that I decided to purchase a home in the neighborhood that I was living in. This decision was fueled by the fact that I had just gotten a promotion, so of course, the Upgrade Cycle took its psychological effect—my pay increase was approximately $700 monthly, and it was just waiting to be spent; I was pretty excited that I could now purchase a home.

I began thinking through all the reasons why I shouldn't be renting, just as many people do—what if the homeowners wanted to move back in, displacing my family; what if the property manager decided to raise the rent; why was *I* not taking advantage of building equity, everyone else was doing it; and so what *if* I couldn't sell my home in two years—I would just rent it out, and so on. After all was said and done, I made the decision to "stop throwing my money away" and went for the home purchase. It was a win for me, or so I thought. Did I really stop throwing my money away?

Conveniently enough, the home that I decided to purchase was the same exact home that I had been renting, with only a few differences. The purchased home was only six homes away, about a quarter of a mile down the same street. Both homes were side-by-side townhomes in a golf community. Both homes had three bedrooms and two bathrooms. Additionally, both homes were approximately 1800 square feet, ranch-style, with a one-car garage. In fact, with the exception of a fireplace, appliances, and the type of carpet, the purchased home that I decided to buy was basically identical to the rental.

The final mortgaged amount for my home was $193,865. And unfortunately for me, I mortgaged my home –like the many others who *prevent wealth*--using a thirty-year fixed rate at 6.5%. In contrast to renting, and contrary to the idea that I would "stop throwing my money away," as soon as I signed on the dotted line, I started "throwing my money away."

When I was renting essentially the same exact home, my rent was only $1,000 monthly, nothing more, nothing less. As soon as I signed my loan papers, my mortgage was a fixed payment of $1225.36. Immediately, I was paying $225.36 more than what I was paying when I was a renter—but I was "building equity." Furthermore, as opposed to when I was renting, I now had to pay property taxes and home owner's insurance. The taxes and homeowner's insurance added an additional monthly amount to the mortgage payment, and it totaled about $268.12. So I was immediately now paying $493.48 more than when I was renting.

To be fair, when I was renting I did have the additional expense of renter's insurance—this policy was approximately $20.00 monthly. But when I became a homeowner, even that amount was a pittance as compared to the monthly flood insurance premium that I began paying. Although I had gotten rid of my renter's insurance, I began paying $27.25 monthly for flood insurance. Still, it did not stop there.

As a renter, I was not responsible for paying the homeowner's association yearly fees. And although I did not have to pay the fees, my family and I had the same privileges as every homeowner in the neighborhood without paying anything; they were included in the rent. My family had access to the community pool and the parks, and our landscape was taken care of just like every other home. But when I became a homeowner, the privileges were no longer "free." I inherited the fees, and they were an additional $845 per year—$845 that I didn't have to pay as a renter. In terms of a monthly payment, it was an additional $70.40. So all in all, the privilege of home ownership added an additional $571.13 per month to my expenses!

As explained by the Upgrade Cycle, it was really quite expected—the money would have gone somewhere, why not put it on a house? What did I really gain? I had successfully negated the increase in my pay by simply transferring it to our new home. I was now effectively bringing home the same amount of monthly income as I was before my promotion.

Rent	$1000	Principal Payment*	$175.26
Renter's Insurance	$20.00	Interest*	$1050.10
		Escrow	$268.12
		HOA fees	$70.40
		Flood Insurance	$27.25
Total Renting:	**$1020.00**	**Total Buying:**	**$1591.13**
Difference: $571.13			

*Interest payments decrease and principal payments increase over the life of the loan

Am I really building equity?

Still, one would probably argue, "But you're building home equity." Am I? After five years of paying the mortgage, using a thirty-year mortgage at 6.5%, the equity built in the home would be only $12,386.19, assuming that the home's value does not change. But, if I would have kept the extra $571.13 monthly, and put it into a savings account, my liquid savings, or real money, would have grown to $34,267.80 in that same five years! In effect, renting would have not thrown my money away, but allowed me to grow a substantial savings with fewer financial obligations with respect to owning a home.

Year	Total Payments	Principal Paid	Interest Paid	Ending Principal Balance
				$193,865.00
1	$14,704.32	$2,166.91	$12,537.41	$191,698.09
2	$14,704.32	$2,312.02	$12,392.30	$189,386.07
3	$14,704.32	$2,466.86	$12,237.46	$186,919.21
4	$14,704.32	$2,632.05	$12,072.27	$184,287.16
5	$14,704.32	$2,808.35	$11,895.97	$181,478.81

To be fair, if I were to assume that the home's value increased, the results would be much different. At a modest estimated rate of growth of 4% per year for five years, the home's value would grow to $235,866.44. This would give me home equity of $54,729. Unfortunately one thing has to be noted: A 4% home growth rate is not guaranteed. But what would have been guaranteed is at least $34,267.80 of liquid savings in a savings account.

Future Value of Property if

Grown at 4% Annual for Five Years

$$\$193,865 \times 1.04^5 = \$235,866.44$$

So was I really throwing my money away by renting? "Yes," says the stubborn and ill-informed consumer, "I'll never see the rent money again." But if we breakdown our mortgage payment more, we'll soon see that there is plenty of money that I'll never see again. In fact, my payment of $1225.36 is made up of an interest payment to the bank and a principal payment to the loan. Specifically, my first payment was $1050.10 in interest with only $175.26 going towards "building equity." The interest payment, like my rent, is money that is not going to me or the home, but to the bank. And it is even more than what my rental payment was, and will be greater than my rent for more than forty-seven months! So can't we argue that this money is being throwing away?

Payment Number	Payment (P + I)	Principal	Interest	Ending Principal Balance
				$193,865.00
1	$1,225.36	$175.26	$1,050.10	$193,689.74
2	$1,225.36	$176.21	$1,049.15	$193,513.53
3	$1,225.36	$177.16	$1,048.20	$193,336.37
4	$1,225.36	$178.12	$1,047.24	$193,158.25
5	$1,225.36	$179.09	$1,046.27	$192,979.16
6	$1,225.36	$180.06	$1,045.30	$192,799.10
7	$1,225.36	$181.03	$1,044.33	$192,618.07
8	$1,225.36	$182.01	$1,043.35	$192,436.06
9	$1,225.36	$183.00	$1,042.36	$192,253.06
10	$1,225.36	$183.99	$1,041.37	$192,069.07
11	$1,225.36	$184.99	$1,040.37	$191,884.08
12	$1,225.36	$185.99	$1,039.37	$191,698.09
13	$1,225.36	$187.00	$1,038.36	$191,511.09
14	$1,225.36	$188.01	$1,037.35	$191,323.08
15	$1,225.36	$189.03	$1,036.33	$191,134.05
16	$1,225.36	$190.05	$1,035.31	$190,944.00
17	$1,225.36	$191.08	$1,034.28	$190,752.92
18	$1,225.36	$192.12	$1,033.24	$190,560.80
19	$1,225.36	$193.16	$1,032.20	$190,367.64
20	$1,225.36	$194.20	$1,031.16	$190,173.44
21	$1,225.36	$195.25	$1,030.11	$189,978.19
22	$1,225.36	$196.31	$1,029.05	$189,781.88
23	$1,225.36	$197.37	$1,027.99	$189,584.51
24	$1,225.36	$198.44	$1,026.92	$189,386.07
25	$1,225.36	$199.52	$1,025.84	$189,186.55
26	$1,225.36	$200.60	$1,024.76	$188,985.95
27	$1,225.36	$201.69	$1,023.67	$188,784.26

28	$1,225.36	$202.78	$1,022.58	$188,581.48
29	$1,225.36	$203.88	$1,021.48	$188,377.60
30	$1,225.36	$204.98	$1,020.38	$188,172.62
31	$1,225.36	$206.09	$1,019.27	$187,966.53
32	$1,225.36	$207.21	$1,018.15	$187,759.32
33	$1,225.36	$208.33	$1,017.03	$187,550.99
34	$1,225.36	$209.46	$1,015.90	$187,341.53
35	$1,225.36	$210.59	$1,014.77	$187,130.94
36	$1,225.36	$211.73	$1,013.63	$186,919.21
37	$1,225.36	$212.88	$1,012.48	$186,706.33
38	$1,225.36	$214.03	$1,011.33	$186,492.30
39	$1,225.36	$215.19	$1,010.17	$186,277.11
40	$1,225.36	$216.36	$1,009.00	$186,060.75
41	$1,225.36	$217.53	$1,007.83	$185,843.22
42	$1,225.36	$218.71	$1,006.65	$185,624.51
43	$1,225.36	$219.89	$1,005.47	$185,404.62
44	$1,225.36	$221.08	$1,004.28	$185,183.54
45	$1,225.36	$222.28	$1,003.08	$184,961.26
46	$1,225.36	$223.49	$1,001.87	$184,737.77
47	**$1,225.36**	**$224.70**	**$1,000.66**	**$184,513.07**
48	$1,225.36	$225.91	$999.45	$184,287.16
49	$1,225.36	$227.14	$998.22	$184,060.02
50	$1,225.36	$228.37	$996.99	$183,831.65

This shows that I would have to make forty-seven payments before my interest payment would be less than my rent.

The Tax Deduction Is an Illusion

Even still one would argue, "But what about the interest deduction?" Well, I didn't purchase my home because of an interest deduction and I hope none of us ever will. Contrary to popular belief, in reality, the deduction is not as beneficial as one thinks, it's merely a "bonus" of home ownership. And the interest deduction is only beneficial for those individuals or couples whose itemized deductions exceed the standard IRS deduction. The lower the price paid on a home, the lower the interest payments usually are, and because of this mathematical fact, there is a small chance of eligibility.

Let's assume that during a tax year, I paid $12,537.41 in deductible interest from a mortgage (points, private mortgage insurance, interest, etc.) and that I ended the year with $100,000 in taxable income. Furthermore, I'll assume that my federal filing status was "married filing jointly." This means that the standard deduction that I could choose, which would lower my taxable income is $11,600—for 2011.

If I didn't purchase a home, and assuming that I had no other deductible tax incentives, I would take the $11,600 standard deduction. Subtracting the standard deduction from my taxable income leaves $88,400. This is the amount that I would be taxed on without owning a home. But because I did purchase a home, then I would use the $12,537.41 in deductible interest. Because it is higher than the standard deduction, it would make since to claim the interest accumulated because of my home. Subtracting this from my taxable income of $100,000 leaves $87,462.59.

We Think Renting Is Throwing Away Money

This is the amount that I would be taxed on when owning a home.

In the first case, with a taxable income of $88,400 using the 2011 tax brackets for married filing jointly, and assuming no other deductions, I would have a tax liability of $14,350. In the second case, because I have a home, and using the same tax bracket for married filing jointly and assuming no other deductions, my tax liability would be $14,115.64. The difference in tax liability equals a measly $234.35 in savings!

Married Filing Jointly or Qualifying Widow(er) Filing Status, 2011 Rates
10% on the income between $0 and $17,000
15% on the income between $17,000 and $69,000; plus $1,700
25% on the income between $69,000 and $139,350; plus $9,500.00
28% on the income between $139,350 and $212,300; plus $27,087.50
33% on the income between $212,300 and $379,150; plus $47,513.50
35% on the income over $379,150; plus $102,574.00

[Tax Rate Schedule Y-1, Internal Revenue Code section 1(a)]

Tax Liability Without a Home
$$25\% \times (\$88,400 - \$69,000) = [\$4,850] + \$9,500$$
$$= \$14,350$$

Tax Liability With a Home
$$25\% \times (\$87,462.59 - \$69,000)$$
$$= [\$4,615.65] + \$9,500$$
$$= \$14,115.64$$

150

Where is the real benefit in the tax deduction? We would be paying an extra $571 a month as noted above just to save approximately $200 per year on our taxes. Had my home had a lower annual interest rate, I may not have even paid more than the standard deduction in interest. Would this still be a primary reason to purchase a home? The interest rate deduction, generally, favors those who purchase highly priced homes with huge yearly interest payments; but we already established that interest payments go straight to the institution, not towards principal.

Giving up Our Flexibility

Would one still argue that we're throwing money away if we rent? If so, what about the plenty of other factors? If something breaks when we rent, the landlord pays to fix it. If we don't like our neighbors when we rent, we can move out after the lease is up. If we have to relocate because of a job, we don't have to stress about selling our home. And if we're not obligated to a home, we don't have to end up as a landlord if it doesn't sell. If we're not obligated to a home that loses value, we won't end up coming out of pocket to try to sell it.

The bottom line is that we should all think twice before we purchase a home if our arguments are that

We Think Renting Is Throwing Away Money

renting is throwing away money. How can we be throwing our money away when we are paying for a service—with more flexibility than home ownership? There are plenty of benefits of renting. Yet, there are so many of us who *prevent wealth* because we purchase homes thinking that we would throw our money away if we didn't buy.

Chapter 12

We Purchase Thirty Year Mortgages

One of the biggest mistakes that we can possibly make is to purchase a home with a thirty-year mortgage or longer. This drastically prevents our wealth—and it has brought me a great financial loss. It was not until this loss that I actually realized how greatly of a mistake I'd made. If there was ever a time that we prevent wealth in a financial transaction, it's when we begin our loan application process for a mortgage. Like cars, we purchase homes totally backwards—figuring what we want to buy first, and then figuring out how we are going to pay for it later. Once we are emotionally attached, it's too late to reverse the process. So we pay for this mistake heavily and on a large financial scale.

Purchasing a home should be one of the most careful and considered processes that we undertake. Before we even start looking at houses, we should already have an idea of how much we are willing to spend monthly, but if we want to minimize how much wealth we prevent, we need our payment to be within reason, and use a mortgage term of fifteen years or less, with a fixed annual percentage rate. The mortgage term that we select directly affects how much interest we will pay and how long it would take us to build a reasonable amount of equity over the life of our loan.

The thirty-year mortgage has unfortunately somehow been accepted as normal. And as long as this is so, home builders will command their high prices, because they know that they are "reasonable" as long as the money can be obtained through "normal" financing in our society. The question we should be asking, though, is, "This financing is most desirable for whom?" To that I'll answer "the lender," because it is certainly not desirable for us.

We have to first establish the fifteen-year or less mortgage constraint if we want to save money on our home purchases, and we should not look at houses prior to establishing this. We must know our limits, and stay within them. If we can't afford the payments with a fifteen-year mortgage term, but we want to be smart about our finances, then it is best for us to hold off until we can actually purchase a home within this constraint. Doing so saves us tens of thousands of dollars, and helps us build thousands more in equity as compared to a thirty-year mortgage.

Unfortunately, too many of us shop to the contrary. When we do not use such a constraint, we are no longer buying with financial intelligence, but with emotions and desires. If we look for homes without first setting our

154

budgets based on short-term, fixed-rate mortgages, we may easily fall in love with a home that we cannot afford, and that is not within the fifteen year constraint.

Now that we live in world where extended loan terms are what's "normal," we will find that we'll easily accept the longer terms so that we can purchase our home. It is in the bank's best financial interest to give us longer terms. There are even forty and fifty year term mortgages now. The longer the terms that we finance, the more interest we pay over the life off the loan. And even if we don't keep the loan through the full term, which most people do not, in the end, the longer the terms that we finance, the less equity that we will have when we eventually try to sell our home.

Suppose that a home is valued and can be purchased for $200,000, and this so happens to be a home that we have truly fallen in love with. Suppose further that the prevailing interest rates are 6.25 % for a fifteen-year fixed mortgage and 6.5% for a thirty-year fixed mortgage. The monthly mortgage payments are $1,714.85 and $1,264.14, respectfully. Because we are in love with the home, and see that our monthly payments are over $450 more with a fifteen-year fixed payment, emotions and our wealth preventing sense will make the thirty-year fixed term seem more attractive. However, while it is true that there is a big difference of $450 between the two, the power of this example lies in the total interest paid and the equity that is built over the life of the loans.

Over the life of the thirty-year fixed mortgage, we will pay a total of $255,088 in just the interest, and a total of $455,088 for the home! But over the life of the fifteen-year fixed mortgage, we would pay only $108,672 in interest, and only a total cost of $308,672! For an extra $450 per month, we would save ourselves $146,416 over a lifespan of thirty years, and have a home paid in full fifteen years earlier than with the thirty year mortgage! Somehow we are not convinced, and we convince ourselves that the savings are insignificant because we may only be in the home for a short period. But this is when the information is most compelling, which leaves me to my own personal situation.

Mortgage Summary – Thirty Year Fixed	
Loan amount	$200,000.00
Term	30 years
Interest rate	6.500%
Monthly payment (PI)	$1,264.14
Total principal and interest payments	$455,085.82
Total interest	$255,085.82

Mortgage Summary – Fifteen-Year Fixed	
Loan amount	$200,000.00
Term	15 years
Interest rate	6.250%
Monthly payment (PI)	$1,714.85
Total principal and interest payments	$308,671.62
Total interest	$108,671.62

When I purchased my home, it was definitely a "wealth preventing" transaction. I purchased it with a 100% no-money-down loan, and my mortgage was a thirty-year fixed rate at 6.5%. The purchase price was approximately $193,500 with a monthly payment of "only" $1,223.05. Like most people, the $1,223.05 monthly payment was far more attractive than paying the fifteen year payment of

We Purchase Thirty Year Mortgages

$1,659.11. Boy, was I well on my way to preventing wealth.

Unfortunately, and well out of my control, the home values in my area had dropped significantly after my purchase. Approximately three years after purchasing my home for $193,500, an appraisal established my home value at only $171,000! My plans that I had to sell my home were practically shattered. At the end of my third year of living in my home, the principal was still at $186,567.45, because I did not pay any extra money towards principal. I would have had to bring over $16,000 of negative equity to sell my home and another 6% ($10,260) or more to cover any real-estate agent fees for both myself and the buyer. And that would have been the case only assuming that my home could have sold for the price at which the appraiser had valued my home. In total, I would have had to bring over $26,000 in cash to closing. I was not prepared to lose $26,000! Needless to say, I have become a landlord.

What if I would have instead mortgaged my home with a fifteen-year fixed mortgage at 6.25%, but still paid no extra money towards principal? At the end of three years, my principal balance would have been only $167,784.45. And at that point, I would have only had to bring a little over $7044.45 in cash to closing, which is most definitely better than the $26,000.

If I would have instead waited five years to sell my home, assuming that it still appraised for $171,000, the difference owed between the two mortgages would have been even more drastic. At year five, my principal on the thirty-year fixed rate mortgage would have been $181,137.39, but only $147,765.79 for the fifteen-year fixed rate mortgage. It's a huge difference in principal owed—$33,371.49! And this is not even considering the fact that after five years, I would only owe ten years more on my mortgage with a fifteen-year loan, but twenty-five years more with the thirty-year loan.

The fifteen-year fixed mortgage, as opposed to the thirty-year fixed mortgage is undoubtedly a way to build and accumulate wealth, instead of preventing it. Yet, we too often take the easy route. We take what's more attractive and what lets us purchase the bigger home. And millions of us are feeling the pains of it.

One pervasive argument that is often brought up is that we can get the same results if we simply add the $450.00 as an extra payment on the thirty-year fixed rate as if we were paying a fifteen-year fixed rate mortgage. This argument suggests that we would at least be given the flexibility to "back off" of the payments if we need the extra money. The problem with this is that we know ourselves all too well, and we can't honestly say that we will consistently pay the additional amount towards principle each month. If we could, we would simply get a fifteen-year term in the beginning.

We somehow find something to do with the money, or the money finds something to do with us. Perhaps we'll lose it in the Upgrade Cycle and purchase a new car. Or maybe we'll decide that the money is best used to purchase new clothes, we would or dine out more often. The reality is that chances are we'll never commit to the extra payments if we talk ourselves out of doing it in the beginning.

But if we are consistent, the argument is correct. Once again, let us use as an example, the $200,000 thirty year, 6.5% fixed rate loan. Assuming we prepay an extra $450 monthly, starting at our first payment, we would save over $137,878.26 over the life of the loan.

Prepayment Summary for the Original $200,000 Loan	
Amount	$450.00 Monthly
Start with payment	1
Total payments	$317,207.56
Total interest	$117,207.56
Interest savings	$137,878.26

Still, another argument that we may run into is one that tells us to get the longest mortgage rate available and invest the difference for an even higher return than what we'll pay in interest. My question is where can we put $450.00 a month and *guarantee* even a consistently modest 6.5% annual return over thirty years? In theory, the argument is correct, but no one can guarantee this type of return. However, what we can guarantee is that with a 6.25% fixed rate fifteen-year mortgage we'll save over $146,000 and have a paid-off home in only fifteen years, subsequently guaranteeing us over $1700 per month in our pockets if we decide to stay in our home after it is paid for free and clear.

What other compelling evidence can exist that could convince us otherwise? I wish that I had someone beating this chapter into my ears when I decided to purchase my first home. Instead, I am now saving expeditiously to refinance my home, curtailing every expense that is not a necessity to make the refinance happen sooner rather than later. Why should I continue to prevent wealth? Why should we prevent wealth?

Chapter 13

We are Horrible Investors

How much money have you lost in the "market" by purchasing individual stocks? How about mutual funds? I can tell you that for me, it's been more than I would have liked. Of course we all should know that investing in the "markets" has both advantages and disadvantages. And each thing that we choose to invest in carries its own unique level of risk. Generally speaking, most stocks are more risky than mutual funds, and mutual funds are more risky than most bonds, and so on and so on. I will assume that if you've ever put a dollar in the stock market, whether in bonds or stocks, you already know this much.

Interesting enough, despite the fundamental risk hierarchy described above, many of us begin active investing by ourselves with only this knowledge and nothing more. Discount brokerage firms have made it relatively easy for the average person actively invest; we are enticed by advertisements all the time. In most cases, because these firms exist to make a profit, there is usually no guided help. Or even if there were help, we would most like determine that we wouldn't need it, because for some reason we would decide that we know exactly what we're doing—despite the odds that are stacked against us—and we would conclude that we can outdo the "experts. All we would need for a boost of confidence is the perpetually placed advertisements, news, or peers who tout that we should "just invest." And after we see that we have the extra funds to do so, we'll "go all in" with the desire to strike it rich.

We begin by transferring our initial deposit into our brokerage account that conveniently enough, was set up for free. We may have an idea of where we want to invest, but in most cases we don't. All that we really know is that we are ready to invest in something. So what do we do? We purchase the first stock that we believe is going to do well. Then we purchase the next one, and then the next one until our portfolios are filled with the greatest stock picks ever. If we are savvy enough, we even make sure that we've got a little diversification going on. What degree of diversification we have going on, who really knows? We just suppose that as long as one stock is not in the same sector as another, we're sufficiently diversified—done. And then we just wait for the magic to happen.

We use either our discount brokerages' Web site or some online portfolio program to watch the value of our stocks daily. When we see the value going up, we are overcome with excitement; when we see the value going down, we are overcome with concern. We follow the news and listen to the pundits and the experts who tell us the predicted trends of our stocks. If we like what we hear, we purchase more shares. If we don't like what we hear, we sell our shares.

If it's not enough to listen to the news, we may attempt our own research. We find ourselves in the "expert" analysis section of our brokerage account's Web site, and we see the three experts that recommend the buy, and the three experts that recommend the sell. Confused by the split analysis, we are "stock-locked" at this point, so we now have to do more research on the Internet. We stumble upon other experts on other "expert" news sites who only add to the confusion as some of these expert analyzers also recommend a buy, while some of them recommend selling. After tallying the numbers, we find that there are more buy recommendations in the "buy pool" than in the "sell pool," so we settle on the buy recommendations, and feel just a tad bit better about our stock purchases and eventually stay with them—life is good.

Just when we thought things were on the up-and-up, some perceived negative event comes out looming large in the news about one of the companies in which we just so happened to have invested money. And like so many before us have done, we react, which is called behavioral investing—not financial analysis investing. We hurry to sell, and we pull out of the market. If we are lucky, we realize a small gain— however, we think nothing about the tax implications. If we are not so lucky, we just count our losses as long as we are not the sucker that rides the company's stock down to the bottom. So far, we're happy at this point that we've lost only a few bucks, including some to cover our buying and selling fees. But wait. During the beginning of the next week, we will hear a report on the news that the company's stock that we've just sold off is now recovering. After just a few days into the next week, the stock is once again higher than the previous week's market low. It is at this point that we kick ourselves, and we vow to never again be so reactive to market news—until next time, when the cycle starts all over again with the other stocks in our portfolio.

If you've paid any attention to the above scenario, you would understand that one out of many important aspects of stock picking was missing—the financial analysis! Too many of us purchase stocks, mutual funds, or any other type of investment just as described. I know I have. We hear that a company has a hot new product coming out so we jump right into the stock—never mind the financial health of the company or the research to determine the competition within the market in which the company operates.

Behavioral and speculative type "investing" is manifested in many of our attitudes. Armed without the prerequisite knowledge of fundamental investing and with the lack of a questioning attitude, we sufficiently succeed in preventing wealth. "This knowledge is not required," says a friend of mine. "If you are not taking chances, then you'll never be rich." Unfortunately, this is the attitude of the majority of us "small time" investors—we too often speculate. We've had no official—or unofficial—education in investing. We're unwilling to educate ourselves using sufficient and relevant educational market sources, and don't really understand what we get ourselves into. Yet, we decide that we are well-off enough to put our money in the stock market. I mean, how else are we going to get rich, right?

Even still, if it were as easy as making well-informed and educated decisions to pick stocks, then shouldn't most every person with a degree specialization in financial management or who carries the Chartered Financial Analysis specialization be a millionaire? If the truth is told, all of them are not—and I bet few of them are.

And if they are millionaires, you better believe it's from "managing" other people's money, not necessarily their own. The point is that it takes time, energy, education, dedication, a stomach for risk and many other things to "hit it big" in individual stock investing. Even when that day comes, one has to strategically time—if that's even possible—when they should "pull out" of their investments to actually realize the gain.

What about mutual funds?

While in general, mutual funds are safer investments than stocks, and does not require us to be as actively invested in our investments like individually held stocks, it is not true in every case. We can easily become overwhelmed by the number of mutual funds available on the market. Just think about it. Just about every financial institute has its own family of mutual funds. Additionally, most financial institutes that have their own mutual funds allow you to purchase the funds of other financial institutes if they have a brokerage service. So then the question becomes whose funds should I buy?

We would hope that purchasing mutual funds would be as easy as answering the question above, but unfortunately it is not. We still have to know the type of fund in which we want to invest. There are equity funds, bond funds, money market funds, hedge funds, exchange-traded funds, and even funds of funds. Within these types of funds are loaded funds and non-loaded funds, growth funds and value funds, actively-managed funds, index funds, and so on. And of course, each fund that we purchase has its own expenses.

Many funds have management fees, service fees, investor fees, and commission pay outs. We would hope that the fees would be standard, but as we may know, they vary. Even the same type of fund at one investment company may have a different fee structure than the same type of fund at another investment company.

So although mutual funds are in general, safer than individual stocks, we prevent wealth by investing in these vehicles, just like in stocks, without the knowledge to make a truly informed decision. Let's take for example any fund that we may have in our portfolio. Do we know the top ten stocks or bonds held in our fund? Do we know how much the management fees are or whether we are paying additional expenses that we weren't told about? Do we know the objective that the fund manager has set for the fund? Although we may not know off hand, shouldn't we at least know where to look to find this information?

There was an article run by National Public Radio and written by John Ydstie called, "401(k)s Still Fall Short as a Retirement Strategy."[ii] A 401(k) generally invests in mutual funds that are managed by an outside brokerage fund. In the article, Ydstie shows that a 1979 $10,000 initial investment in the S&P 500 with no fees would have grown to $427,843.12 in December 2009. However, with just 2% in fees, this same investment would have grown to only $202,571.16! More than half of a person's investment can be absorbed by fees alone, over a fairly long investment period. There are many questions that we probably should know before we even begin investing in the relatively "safer" mutual funds.

We haven't even begun to talk about investing timelines or how much risk we are willing to accept—even when purchasing mutual funds. On top of all the fees that we may pay, we can lose plenty of money investing in mutual funds. For example, if you were invested in an index fund that followed the S&P 500 in 2008, you may have lost over 37% of your fund's value in that year had you pulled your money out! The good news is that in 2009 the same fund may have returned over 27%, but would that have helped you if you had already pulled your money out the prior year?

We must know the cost of any underlying mutual fund that we invest in. We must, at a minimum read through our fund's prospectus. The prospectus is one of the most valuable tools that you can read when it comes to researching where to put our money. They report the funds risks, give a recommended investing timeline, and answer many other important questions that we may have before we genuinely commit ourselves to a specific mutual fund.

So what about bonds?

My favorite story about bonds comes in the form of an interview that I gave to a student applying for a business program. I asked the student, what was the last thing that he'd read regarding business, formally in a book or informally over the Internet? The student's response was, "I recently read a book about bonds and how they are the safest investment tools available."

My face just lit up in an infuriating glow. I don't know whether it was because I thought that the student was lying to me about the reading or if the student truly believed that this was true. So, of course my follow-up question was, "What about junk bonds?" With no shame, the student repeated, "Yes, even junk bonds are one of the safest investments one can make." I wanted to hang my head in shame for this student.

Just like stocks or mutual funds, or any type of investing vehicle, bonds are plentiful and also have their own inherited risks. But we make them sound so inviting by calling them, "high-yield bonds" instead of "higher-risk bonds." Fortunately for us, there are research companies such as Moody's, S&P, and Fitch that report the supposedly unbiased risks of bonds by using a rating system. But, how many of us use these ratings that the research companies provide prior to purchasing our bonds? Do we know the meaning of each rating that the research companies provide? Are we purchasing "highly speculative bond investments" or in other words, "junk bonds?"

So although bonds are relatively safe, we still should not invest blindly. Even treasury bonds that are supposedly "risk-free"—because they are backed by the full faith of the United States government—can one day be at risk for default given the current uncertain trend in the United States' economy. Have we thought about this before deciding to put our money in bonds?

If a bond is offering a particularly high return rate, we owe it to ourselves to figure out why. What are the implications of purchasing the bond? What are the risks involved? Specifically, what is the default risk, or how likely a company is to defaulting on their debts, before we sell off our bonds?

Investing 101

We somehow manage to purchase bonds without knowing the meaning of their ratings, mutual funds without ever looking into the prospectus—or knowing what it is—and stocks without knowing what a financial statement is. And because we do this, once again, we are already destined to fail—unless we really do catch a lucky speculative break. On top of this knowledge deficiency, we don't ask any other important questions about our investment choices. If we are to accumulate wealth instead of prevent it, we have to understand where, why, and how we invest.

If we are to build wealth by investing in the "markets," then we must learn what we are investing our money in. If there were ever a tine that we needed to be skeptical about our purchases, it's when we commit to investment vehicles that are set up to secure our financial future. We may not be able to learn all the details of investing, but we owe it to ourselves to understand where we, or someone who manages our money is putting it, and how much it will cost us. We should know the general differences between passive and active investing, how to compare financial statements, or how to find and understand the total amount, including expenses and fees, that our investments ultimately cost us. We owe ourselves the education to make smart, well-informed decisions, so that we do not prevent our wealth.

Chapter 14

We Don't Prepare for the Unexpected

If we were to count, how many people do we think we can come up with that have been caught off guard by some unexpected financial disaster? How many people were ready to face the devastation of Hurricane Katrina in 2005, or Hurricane Andrew in 1992? What about the floods in the Millington, Tennessee area in 2009? What about any other natural disaster? There are blizzards, thunderstorms, floods, hail storms, tornados, earthquakes, and other natural disasters that none of us have any control over. If we're lucky, we may find out about a disaster before it hits so that we may escape unscathed, but will our homes be protected?

What would happen if our spouses unexpectedly passed away? Will we be prepared? Have we thought about this at all? Shouldn't the non-working spouse be covered by insurance in some form or fashion? How would it affect our incomes if the spouse who stays at home to take care of several children is no longer available to do so? Will the working spouse have to quit their job? If so, how will income be earned?

What would we do if all of a sudden our car broke down and we needed it fixed right away? What if we were in the middle of a term paper for an online class when all of a sudden our computer crashed? Worse yet, would we be able to pay for a flight for the family if we needed to attend a distant funeral? Would we resort to credit cards to cover these unexpected events?

How about the protection of our incomes? What means of protection have we established if we were to become disabled? What if we were to be laid off of work? How long would we be able to pay our bills? Have we even thought about this?

Unfortunately, too many of us do not prepare for the unexpected. Things happen all the time that are beyond our control, but it is up to us to protect ourselves, or we might end up becoming victims of our own demise when an event threatens our standards of living.

Protecting ourselves is all about crisis and risk management. If we lose our income—a crisis—we should have a back-up plan to offset the severity. If our home is destroyed in a storm, we shouldn't have to worry; we should know that we're protected.

All of the questions I've asked are probably things that we have had happen to us or to someone close to us. I had a friend whose home was flooded in New Orleans during Hurricane Katrina and also knew of several people whose homes were flooded in 2010 during the rain storm in

Millington, Tennessee. Fortunately some were protected, but unfortunately, others were not. How would we have handled the crisis? For all of the reasons above, we need to have crisis mitigation plan, which comes in the form of emergency savings accounts, and by having different types of insurance protections.

Emergency Savings Accounts

An emergency savings account helps us combat short-term hiccups and undoubtedly helps to keep us from *preventing wealth* in the process. There are an unfortunate number of us who simply suggest that we should use a credit card in the event of an emergency, but does this make financial sense? If we have to use credit cards when an emergency happens, because we don't have the cash on hand, we may find ourselves with yet another payment that we can't afford. We should set an effective goal to save a specific total amount that we are comfortable having in an account solely for an emergency. The funds in an emergency account should be able to pay a set number of months' worth of living expenses, repair an unexpected failure of an appliance or car, or fly a family to an unexpected funeral, if necessary. We must make it a priority to have an emergency fund.

We Don't Prepare For the Unexpected

Whatever it takes, we have to always prepare ourselves for short-term emergencies. If our washing machine fails, we should be able to go into a liquid account, take from it to fix or replace our machine, and rest easy knowing that we don't have to *prevent wealth* by borrowing from a creditor and paying them interest. And it should go without saying that we would need to consistently build the emergency fund back up so that we are protected during the inevitable next event.

Life Insurance

One of the most important insurance policies that anyone with others depending on their income should have is life insurance. How many of us have such a policy, and how much do we need? At its most basic level, our life insurance policies should be adequate enough to cover our financial debts and maintain the same standard of living for our families when we pass. So instead of covering ourselves in this case, we are protecting our families from the unexpected. At a relatively low cost, is there any reason why we shouldn't pay approximately $30 a month to have $300,000 worth of coverage for twenty years?

Life insurance helps our families to survive if we pass our debts on to them when we pass away. If we don't expect our spouses to work now because they are taking care of children, why should they have to both work and take care of the children when we pass? Why should we leave them to worry when we can have an insurance policy that can be used to pay off a home mortgage, fully fund our children's college expenses, and pay off all of our other debts? Yet, there are so many of us who do not take advantage of life insurance policies that prepare our families for the unexpected.

Property Insurance

How would we handle the situation if our home was suddenly swept away in a tornado? Or what would we do if a fire started in our home? What about if it were burglarized? It would be nice if an emergency fund could cover every event, but for issues such as these, it probably wouldn't. Fortunately for us, these events could be covered by a risk transferee, an insurance company.

Many of us do not have the money on hand to fix our homes if a tree falls through the roof, or to replace our $2,000 DVD collection when a "friend" steals them from our room; even if we have the money, it may be something that we would not want to pay for out-of-pocket in full. Because of this, we should have adequate insurance to pay for these unfortunate events. If we do not, our savings can easily be wiped clean. I couldn't imagine trying to pay for content replacement in an apartment if it were flooded or caught fire. While such events are unlikely to happen, there is no guarantee that they won't happen. We don't have much control over these events, but we can be protected if they occur. We don't have to let unfortunate events become our financial demise. Property insurance, whether it is for a home or apartment that we are renting, or for a home that we own, protects us from theft, fire, burglary, or any natural calamity like tornados, earthquakes, or floods. For a relatively low price, we can't afford not to have it.

Disability, Health, Auto, and other Insurance

Just as there is insurance for homes and apartments, there is insurance to provide protection for our incomes (disability insurance), our health (medical insurance), and of course, our vehicles. There is also another type of insurance that protects us from damage that we may cause to others. Like other types of insurance, they require a co-pay or deductible, but that payment will pale in comparison in the event that we did not have insurance. Some people consider health insurance as too expensive, but when we only have to pay $500 per month to protect us from paying $50,000 for a procedure, or monthly payment will quickly become the best money that we could have spent.

Do You Have Enough Insurance?

Even if we have insurance, is it enough? Most homes are protected by homeowner's insurance if they're mortgaged, but does the policy cover only the minimum just to "check the box?" Does the apartment's rental insurance cover the full replacement value of our belongings? Does the policy cover hotel expenses if we needed to vacate our homes because of a repair that is covered by the insurance company? All of these are questions that we should ask when selecting a policy so that we can protect our income if an unfortunate event should happen.

Conclusion

There are so many of us who fail to take advantage of an opportunity that prepares us for the unexpected. Despite the relatively low costs to transfer the risk to a company that can actually afford to pay for our unexpected and unfortunate events, we make excuses not to pay for these policies, or we simply do not care or understand the importance. I would argue, however, that we can't afford *not* to pay for them. We should ecstatically pay the relatively low amounts of money to protect us from paying much more than we have to.

Whether we want to accept it or not, catastrophic events happen, and we should always be prepared when we can. Having emergency funds and adequate insurance policies will spare our wealth and will definitely help us more than hurt us. Having these policies established are probably more important than any other component of a sound financial plan, because without these, we may find ourselves in a world of hurt when we are caught unprepared for the unexpected. This will in turn undoubtedly *prevent wealth*.

Chapter 15

We Don't Understand the Importance of Retirement

Savings

It wasn't until recently that I realized how important it was to save, and to do it consistently—I mean, really realize the importance. We hear all the time that we should save for retirement, but what guidance do we have? We should all know the importance of having an emergency savings account. We also should know that we should have some sort of disability insurance to protect us against an income loss if an unfortunate event should happen. Furthermore, we should now know to have enough life insurance so that our dependents may pay off our bills and maintain their same standard of living in the unfortunate event of our death. The thoughts of not having these should be scary enough, but the most compelling thing that scares me is the fact that so many of us don't know or understand the importance of saving for retirement. Even if we do understand the concept, we may not fully understand how to fully assess the amount that we should save.

I first introduced the retirement income calculator concept in chapter 2. The inputs of a retirement income calculator are mainly our savings rate, assumed interest rates on our savings, assumed inflation, tax rates, and our time in years or months until retirement. The corresponding outputs are the assumed results of what our savings will yield, or the income that we would have in retirement on a monthly basis. While it is common to hear the examples that indicate an individual will have X amount of dollars if he or she saves Y amount monthly, it doesn't mean much unless we talk about it in terms of monthly retirement income and compare it to an assumed monthly cost of living. For example, is $1,000,000 enough for retirement at sixty years old? What about $2,000,000? Well, it depends.

Let us revisit an example of inputs from a retirement income calculator. Let us assume that we are thirty years old, with no savings, and that after reading a book on the importance of retirement savings, we begin to save 15% of our monthly income. Let's assume that this turns out to be $250 monthly. As far as we know, by time we reach sixty years old we should be set, right? Of course it depends on the rate that our investment yields, but because we would have thirty-five years until retirement, we'll safely assume again, as in Chapter 2, that our investments will grow at a conservative 6% annually. Taking a 2% inflation rate into consideration, it would roughly grow to, $354,363 using a 25% tax rate. Is this enough? If we take it a step further, assuming only a 15% tax bracket in retirement and that our money will continue to grow at 6% annually, we will have enough to pay us a monthly sum of $2,130 for twenty years. We should be just fine right? Well, there are many assumptions involved in these numbers, and we would reveal that even with these assumptions, the $2,130 will most likely not be enough for us to quit working, assuming that this amount is our only income at retirement.

The first and one of the biggest assumptions, next to the assumed average interest rate is that we will save the $250 per month, consistently for the next thirty years. Talking to people in my peer group, this is unlikely something that someone in his or her thirties does often. There are many excuses why this doesn't occur, and the theme of this book talks about many of them.

A second assumption is that the average return per year for the next thirty years will be 6%. Unfortunately, we've had years where the markets have had both negative and positive returns, and periods where a 6% annual return was only hopeful. In other words, there is no guaranteed of a consistent annual 6% gain in any investment that sells on the stock market. Perhaps, our savings will yield only an average of 6%. But for now, we will stick with our initial assumptions so that we can have a "healthy" nest egg of $354,363 when we hit the age of 65. Is this enough to last us for twenty years? Like I said, it depends.

Retirement Income Results	
Starting Balance	$0
Annual Contribution	$3,000
Current Age	30
Age of Retirement	65
Years of Retirement	20
Rate of Return Before Retirement	6.00%
Rate of Return During Retirement	6.00%
Current Tax Rate	25.00%
Retirement Tax Rate	15.00%
Expected Rate of Inflation	2.00%
Is This Savings Tax Deferred?	Yes
Increase Annual Deposit With Inflation?	No
Total Contributions	$105,000
Savings Total Before Taxes	$354,363
Savings Total After Taxes	$301,208
Value Of Savings Today	$150,612
Savings Can Provide	
Income Before Taxes	$2,506 Per Month
Income After Taxes	$2,130 Per Month
Value Of Income in Today's Dollars (With 2.00% Annual Inflation)	$1,065

According to these inputs, at age sixty-five your savings will provide $2,506 per month for twenty years. This is before taxes. After taxes you will have $2,130 per month. In today's dollars, this is equivalent to $1,065 with 2.00% annual inflation.

How We Prevent Wealth

We cannot tell what future prices in utilities such as water and electricity will be, but let's make a few more assumptions. Let's outlandishly assume that phone bills remain around $100, internet $50, cable $100, electricity $300, water $50, and auto insurance $100. This brings our total utilities to $700. Well, we still have to eat, so we'll assume $300 for groceries for a husband and wife, and because we are retired, we want to splurge and go out to dinner every now and again, spending $100 per month. At this point, we are already at a total of $1,100 monthly. Of course, we still need to purchase items for the house as they are expended such as toilet paper, cleaning supplies, and other things. So, we'll throw in another $100 for a total of $1,200 in monthly bills. This $1,200 doesn't seem bad at all, but we have failed to add in a home mortgage or rent. Hopefully, our homes are paid off in retirement, but let's assume they are not, or that we are renting. A good number to use would be $1,200. This puts our total expenses at $2,224, but our retirement income calculator has already predicted a relatively meager $2,130. Now, did we save enough? Or are we already behind?

As we see, even with our assumed savings and rates of return, our $353,363 can end up being meager financial support. Can we assume that social security will supplement our income? Is our car paid for? What happens if we are paying for a car? What would happen if we have other activities that we enjoy doing? We could maybe take more from our nest egg one year, but wouldn't that affect our retirement income later? Now is our savings enough? I don't think so. And do we really want to continue to work after the age of sixty-five, when we would have been working for already more than thirty-five years?

What's amazing is that many of us start too late and do not allow for compounded interest to work in our favor, which means that if we don't put aside more than a consistent $250 a month when we're older than thirty, we may never have a comfortable nest egg. Where would we even begin trying to find the extra money? By the time we reach thirty years old, we may have already made a lifetime of mistakes that we have to recover from, which means that saving for retirement may become harder as we age.

If we can't find at least $250 monthly for retirement, shouldn't we start taking our consumption more serious now, given this example? We have created so many other obligations and excuses for ourselves, that we can't even meet a savings amount that will generate enough income that sets us free in the end. Why is this? What is preventing us from gaining our freedom?

How We Prevent Wealth

It should be no secret at this point that clearly, even someone who devotes $250 a month for the next thirty years of his or her life may still be working way into their golden years if they start saving too late. The financial utopia will be close, but not close enough. Without running the numbers, it should be evident that the true amount needed in this case would be much more; assuming in retirement that our home is not paid off and that we have other debts.

There is some good news, however. We can always contribute more if we make it a priority to do so or if we start saving at a younger age, say ten years younger. An extra $250 monthly contribution over thirty years may actually give us about $500 more per month in retirement. Once again, any retirement income calculator, like the one on *Bankrate.com's* Web site is a great tool for assessing these values.

The point is that if we truly want to be free financially, we have to realize what it is that prevents us from doing so. Only after we realize how we led ourselves into our self-made pitfalls can we gather the proper motivation to do what is necessary to make smart financial choices a priority. Only after the proper motivation can we truly enjoy life without work, or eventually work only because we truly choose to do so. The outlook is scary, and we need to stop making excuses for ourselves and pass the word to others—even what we are currently saving may not be enough to live comfortably in retirement!

So what are we ultimately aiming for? To start, *wealth building* is a long-term process of making the right choices and holding ourselves accountable for our poor choices. In the end, everyone's definition of wealth is different, but at a minimum, if we want to truly be free and live life to its fullest in retirement, we have to allow plenty of time for compounded interest to work for us or be forced to save much more money later in life; we have to do one or the other. We can choose to do the right thing and minimize our sacrifices while we are young, or do the wrong thing and sacrifice greatly when we are older. We have to save the most that we possibly can while simultaneously minimizing, if not eliminating, all debts including a mortgage, so that in our golden years we can choose how we want to spend our time.

The years of the "thirty and out" pension plans are gone. More and more, we are the ones responsible for saving for our retirement. Even if social security is available for us when we are eligible, do we really want to rely on it? Will social security even be enough? We can take our chances, or we can stop *preventing wealth* and focus on maximizing our retirement savings now.

Retirement Income Results	
Starting Balance	$0
Annual Contribution	$3,000
Current Age	20
Age of Retirement	65
Years of Retirement	20
Rate of Return Before Retirement	6.00%
Rate of Return During Retirement	6.00%
Current Tax Rate	25.00%
Retirement Tax Rate	15.00%
Expected Rate Of Inflation	2.00%
Is This Savings Tax Deferred?	Yes
Increase Annual Deposit With Inflation?	No
Total Contributions	**$135,000**
Savings Total Before Taxes	$676,524
Savings Total After Taxes	$575,046
Value of Savings Today	**$235,882**
Savings Can Provide	
Income Before Taxes	$4,785 Per Month
Income After Taxes	$4,067 Per Month
Value Of Income in Today's Dollars (With 2.00% Annual Inflation)	**$1,668**

According to these inputs, at age sixty-five your savings will provide $4,785 per month for twenty years. This is before taxes. After taxes you will have $4,067 per month. In today's dollars, this is equivalent to $1,668 with 2.00% annual inflation.

We Don't Understand the Importance of Retirement Savings

Are You Secured By Social Security?

This following statement was mailed to me on April 17, 2009:

*In **2017** we will begin paying more in benefits than we collect in taxes. Without changes, by **2041** the Social Security Trust Fund will be exhausted and there will be enough money to pay only about **78** cents for each dollar of scheduled benefits. We need to resolve these issues soon to make sure Social Security continues to provide a foundation of protection for future generations.*

> Signed by Michael J. Astrue, Commissioner of Social Security, 2009

Just in case we needed another indication that we should save for our own retirement, there it is, right from the words of the commissioner himself. Every working American has been told this already. I know this because every year we receive a newsletter entitled "Your Social Security Statement."

On April 9, 2010, the numbers were worse! It read:

*In **2016** we will begin paying more in benefits than we collect in taxes. Without changes, by **2037** the Social Security Trust Fund will be exhausted and there will be enough money to pay only about **76 cents** for each dollar of scheduled benefits. We need to resolve these issues soon to make sure Social Security continues to provide a foundation of protection for future generations.*

These successive statements should speak plenty. However, to the commissioner's credit, the newsletter makes another alarming statement:

Social Security is the largest source of income for most elderly Americans today, but Social Security was never intended to be your only source of income when you retire. You also will need other savings, investments, pensions, or retirement accounts to make sure you have enough money to live comfortably when you retire.

I think that it is totally fair that the commissioner makes it a point to basically say, "If you are counting on Social Security alone to have a comfortable retirement, you're going to have a problem."

So Why Should We Care? What Can We Do in Retirement?

It's always good to talk about "true" retirement, but what's the point if we plan on simply hanging around the house when we no longer have to work? Well, for some, that is a great deal. However, I think that retirement would sound much more pleasurable if we were to imagine what we would do with that time. It compares to the fantasy that many people live every once in a while about winning the lottery. Yet, a "true" retirement has far better odds—and we are the ones in control. So what can we do? Here are three thoughts:

- **Spend more time with the family:** Right now, many of us have to balance work, school, family, and self. With work gone, we would be able to distribute more time to fishing or playing sports with our children or grandchildren, or attend more dating events with our spouses.

- **Learn another language:** I'm not just talking Rosetta Stone® here, but actually spending time in another country interacting with its citizens.

- **Play more video games:** Hey, I have to admit that I enjoy playing video games. I was born in the eighties, which means that many people around my age grew up playing video games, and many of us still do as adults. It takes a good week of continuous play these days to actually master (receive all awards) a game. So, not working will definitely free up time to master more games.

There are many other things that I would do, but these are just some of them. What would you do?

Conclusion

It is important for us to save for our retirement as early and often as possible—we can't afford not to do so. We should all strive to pay ourselves first set an effective goal towards saving for retirement after understanding the basics of investing, regardless of our debt situation. We can always make more money, but we can never get back lost time that could have been used to allow our money to grow.

We Don't Understand the Importance of Retirement Savings

Chapter 16

We're on Different Financial Pages than our Significant

Other

Next to sex, I am willing to bet that the most fought about thing in many relationships is finances. It probably doesn't matter who makes more than whom either. In many relationships, there probably exists a situation where one person is a spender and the other is a saver. Aside from the financial implications of this scenario, relationships involving two people with different ideas about money will rarely work out to be healthy relationships. I've known couples who were heavily in debt, but despite the motivation of one of the partners to shed off debt, the other would just add more debt at the same rate that it was being paid off.

In other scenarios, maybe there are two savers, or two spenders, but one of them is just more extreme than the other. What if one spouse is extremely intense about saving money and wants to put away $500 a month, but can only put away $400 a month because the other spouse has decided that they value collectable dolls more than they value putting away that extra $100? Or maybe there is one person in the relationship who is a heavy charity donator or tither. While one person believes that $500 in weekly tithes is important and fundamental to continued financial blessings, the other may feel that having $500 to be used for discretionary spending *is* the blessing, and should be contributed to a retirement account. Although savings in both situations is occurring, unless there is a compromise, these situations may still lead to *preventing wealth* if they lead to never-ending fights, unhappiness, or even worse, a divorce.

Being on different financial pages can make any relationship grow sour quickly—this is an addition to the normal everyday complaints. So in the end, "money fights" usually pour fuel on top of small fires until they get out of hand. We'll try and try to extinguish these fires, but often with little success.

An unhappy relationship may lead us into trying to buy the happiness of our spouse, when in fact "things" are unlikely to make the relationship better; things would most likely accumulate more debt. If we are unhappy, maybe we'll spend lots of time away from home not working, but in bars or "hanging with the guys or girls." Many people may shop more to overcome a stressful relationship, or travel more often than usual—all leading to an eventual trial separation or divorce—and it should be pretty obvious how these situations *prevent wealth*. If there is a separation phase, both parties accumulate bills that have to be paid, whether or not both parties are working. If there is a divorce, legal fees, possible alimony payments, child-support payments, and split assets will be pursued.

Each couple's situation is unique. The above scenarios involved money fights from savers. In addition to the scenarios above, there are couples who are completely engulfed in debt, yet one spouse wants to remain a spender and is unwilling to accept the reality of the need to reduce spending. Also, there are situations in which the household income is high, but is insignificant when taking into account the spending habits of one or both of the spouses. And then there is the case that my spouse and I had gone through.

The Saver vs. the Non-Saver

I have always tried to be an extreme saver. When I say extreme, I mean so extreme that early into our relationship I would get upset that my spouse would throw away pennies. In the beginning of our relationship, I would always put us on a budget for everything. I would have a set spending budget for gas, groceries, utilities, and more. It was so extreme that even if she wanted something at the grocery store, if it wasn't on the list, I would convince her not to get it because "we were on a budget." I can clearly remember her usual mock, "budget, smudget."

In my mind, it was necessary for this type of restrictive spending. We had come into the marriage with debt just like many young couples, and we accumulated more debt as our marriage matured. But although we had debts, I also wanted us to save. It wasn't much that I wanted to save, but in my spouse's eyes savings for the sake of saving generated no interest—especially if it restricted her from having a nice living or dining room set, or car. Short-term savings was okay, but to hoard money was unacceptable.

But the restrictive attitude of the saver can only hold up for so long. A dilemma is presented; whether to save as much as one can or give a little, through compromise, and spend money to make both spouses happy. If one knows what is best, the choice to make both spouses happy, through compromise, is most often the best choice.

Fortunately for me, my spouse had never been a big spender so the choice to spend more money to make her happy was an easy one—sometimes. Still, when we bought her new cars or clothes or whatever, that was money that we did not save in a retirement or savings account. While saving $500 a month would have made me happy, I know it would not have made a difference to my spouse. So instead, I chose to make her happy and did what every married couple should theoretically do, which is to save and share our money through compromise. But, this was not always easy. I had been the sole "bread winner" for the length of our marriage, and because of this my attitude on spending was usually always the most dominant.

Even though we earned a fairly decent household salary, things were still stressful in terms of spending money. Because I was a saver, the wants of my spouse became insignificant no matter how small they were. There were times where I could never justify why we would need to "upgrade" our comforter set, purchase more school clothes for our son, or purchase a new book bag or lunch box for a new school year when he had already had one. I wouldn't want to spend as much money as she would want for Christmas or birthday presents either, although it wasn't much more than we were going to spend anyway. In most cases she simply gave up because she knew that she would not be able to convince me to spend the extra money, or she knew that a conversation would end up in a money-fight with me telling her in so many words that I was the bread winner and what I said stood.

So what's the right answer and how does this type of attitude prevent us from building wealth? The most obvious answer is that the two conflicting spending habits can eventually get to a point where it is unbearable, and the relationship subsequently grows stale. Instead of enjoying each other's company, money fights will lead to distasteful attitudes that leave the couple not able to stand being with each other.

Either way, unless both people in a relationship are heavy savers and agree upon a savings strategy, someone has to give at his or her own expense. This can be very difficult to do, because it plays on the emotional psyche of the saver. When a spender wants something, without discipline, there is little that their significant other can say or do to stop the spender from buying what he or she wants. And on the contrary, when a saver wants to squeeze in every last penny, because of discipline, there is little the other person can say or do to stop them, unless the spender spends all or most of the money. Either way, someone will be frustrated. Who is right? Is there even a right or wrong person?

Financial Compromises

The only way to combat financial friction in a relationship is through compromise. It is easy in theory, but hard in practice. There are several scenarios in which compromise may work. Let's look at three such scenarios; one scenario involving one working spouse, and the second and third scenarios involving compromises in a two-family income situation.

In the first scenario, there is one working spouse. Regardless of what the non-working spouse does, whether it is because he or she can't find a job or simply desires to stay home with the kids, a compromise between the two workers has to be ascertained. This compromise comes in the form of agreeing upon how to split discretionary income between each member in the family. For this to happen, both people in the relationship have to first sit down and discuss how much money is coming in and how much money is going out. Chances would have it that one of the two don't really care, but sitting down and discussing incomes and outgoes gives a chance for questions to come up and expenses to be clarified. If after the conversation it is determined that there is no discretionary income available, perhaps the spender will scale back his or her spending—hopefully. However, if it is determined that there is, say $1,000 a month for discretionary spending, compromises should then be made.

After determining what's available for discretionary spending, the question between the couple should be, "How are we going to split our discretionary spending so that it is fair for the both of us?" In the best scenario, amounts should be determined and then split between saving and spending. For example, $500 monthly could be saved while $500 monthly is split between the two partners, giving them each $250, as spending money. If one person needs more money and it is mutually agreed upon, maybe it could be worked out that $500 monthly is saved and one person receives $200 monthly to spend while the other gets $300 monthly. In either case, boundaries should be established and both parties should be free to spend without one person scrutinizing the purchases of the other. If it must be done, split the money using cash.

The previous case also works well when both parties are working, which brings us to our second scenario. Despite who makes more than whom, if both partners are working and the salary of one worker is just enough to cover all the household expenses but not save, it is best to use one salary for all household expenses and the other to save and discretionarily spend. The discretionary salary should be split, and just as before, a mutually-agreed-upon amount should be determined such that some is saved and some is spent between the two partners.

In the last scenario, one person makes enough to pay off all of the bills *and* save for the family, but still there are disagreements on how much they should save. For example, I was at a point where I had put so much into savings that I had minimized the amount of spending money between my spouse and me.

I wanted and always will want to save as much as I can for the family because I stress the importance of an early retirement. Consequently, I try to max out our retirement accounts and save intensely for unexpected or irregular expenses that are not in our monthly budget such as yearly homeowner's association dues, life insurance premiums, flood insurance premiums, flights to visit family, random trips, or anything random with our rental home. To me, these are a must, but to my spouse, they were needs, but the importance of how much they were needed was not fully understood. And to me, her attitude was not unacceptable as many may think. In many relationships, one person simple doesn't care as much about finances as the other—it's a fact of life. However, what ended up happening is that the more I saved, the less money remained for my spouse and me to split. Although I was fine with the amount, because savings was my priority for the family, my spouse was not. So in our scenario, and because my son was at an age where my spouse and I were comfortable putting him in an afterschool program, she worked a part-time job. Every penny that she had made was her own to spend. Of course, this is a special case, but it worked for us—we had no debts that we both needed to pay off, and we kept saving at the same rate. I was saving for the family, and my spouse made and spent her own money.

Not every couple can make the compromises that we made, but the point is that one should be made. In certain relationships, one partner would think that it is unfair that one person spends all of "their" money while the other person has to save for both, especially because the savings benefits the two of them. However, the entering argument is that one person is a saver and the other is not. Unless you want to fight about how much you two should save, versus spend, and end up unhappy because of money fights, it is best to let it be, especially if one salary covers expenses and savings goals.

The understanding needs to be that whatever the compromise, money for separate personal spending, that each partner agrees to, should not used to acquire new debt—because ultimately, the debt can become the burden of the both. For example, in our first scenario with one working partner, let us say that between the two partners $250 each was agreed upon for spending money. One partner should not get a credit card or finance a $200 monthly car payment. It has to be understood that the split money is only used for standard expenses.

Once again, whatever the compromise, one has to be made. We cannot build wealth if we are constantly fighting with our significant others about their spending habits. Both partners have to absolutely determine how to spend the house's money. Dealing with an unhappy partner is not fun and divorces are expensive. Most importantly, life is far too short to spend it fighting about money. We should rather spend it accumulating wealth and enjoying each other's company.

We're on Different Financial Pages than our Significant Other

Chapter 17

Our Marriages Often End in Divorce

How many of us know someone whose marriage has ended in divorce? If I were to render a guess, because of the alarming number of marriages that end in divorce, many of us can say we know someone who has gone through one. Even if we end up on the same financial page as our spouses, there are many other things that may pull a relationship apart. Marriages can end in a divorce for many reasons that may include extreme differences in the way children are disciplined, inadequate companionship, sexual infidelity, or simple changes in heart by one or both people in the relationship in general. Whatever the case may be, a divorce will on some level ultimately prevent plenty of wealth.

The most obvious way that a divorce will prevent wealth is the high costs of legal fees involved and then the ultimate division of shared property. Legal fees are additional costs on top of any separation that has taken place prior to a court filing; separations usually consist of both parties paying for a place to live and paying the associated living costs. There are filing fees, mandatory but costly parenting education classes in some states if children are involved, and the cost of individual legal consultation in many cases. In the division of shared property, whether one spouse gets everything or just an equal share, one spouse will usually have to purchase whatever it is that was given up in a settlement. Still, on top of all these costs, some sorts of alimony or child support payments are usually due to one spouse by the other. All the while, this money could have been used to grow a hefty nest egg for the couple.

The loss of income of one of the spouses or the additional expenses that may have to be incurred because a non-working spouse is no longer able to take care of children is an unfortunate reality of a divorce. For example, if one spouse was always accustomed to staying home with the children, but then is awarded custody of the children, whether sole or joint custody was awarded, he or she may now have to pay for the children's care if he or she has to work, because child support may not be enough to support the previous lifestyle.

One sad thing about a divorce is that it is usually predictable in many signs leading up to it. The signs can be blatant or subtle, but the best person who will know what the signs are is one that is in the relationship. Some signs can be noticed if we ask simple questions such as, has one person become emotionally distant, is there an extreme slowdown in communication, has it been communicated that a partner no longer wants to be in a relationship with the other? In any case, the best way to approach any sign is to communicate and seek help early in the difficulty and do the best that we can to save the relationship. Not doing so can result in worse outcomes than we may like.

It can feel quite defeating if after seeking help and doing all that we can to prevent a divorce, efforts still seem to be failing. If the attempts have grown exhaustive, and one person is or both persons are adamant that the relationship will not work, it is usually in the couple's best financial interest to seek an inevitable divorce before things get so bad that malicious acts and dishonesty begin manifesting in the relationship. Staying in a relationship when one person is not wanted by the other, despite all that has been done to keep a relationship strong can make an inevitable divorce worse. If a divorce must happen, it has to be as "cordial" as possible; this will be the only way to minimize how much wealth is ultimately prevented. In other words, it is almost always best to leave a relationship before sexual infidelity or extreme resentment occurs. If not, it will usually make a divorce harder than it already is.

Our Marriages Often End in Divorce

Minimizing the Negative Financial Effects of Divorce

The point of accepting an inevitable divorce early into the signs of emotional withdrawal or before sexual infidelity, knowing that all has been done that can be done (marriage counseling, self-help books, spiritual guidance, etc.), is so that an uncontested divorce can at least be considered, depending on your state's laws. An uncontested divorce is when both spouses agree that the marriage has come to an end and have come to a mutually satisfying agreement regarding a final divorce settlement. Furthermore, both spouses may be able to sit down and agree to a Pro Se divorce litigation. This means that the couple will individually represent themselves, without an attorney, which can cut out expensive attorney fees.

The issue with both an uncontested divorce and a Pro Se divorce litigation is that emotional and legal aspects have to be kept separate. It will be hard to keep these two aspects separated if there is a burning vengeful desire by one spouse because of the acts of the other. In that case, it is always best to seek an attorney. Issues such as dividing marital property, determining alimony, or child support and child custody can come up and can have negative consequences if not properly handled.

How We Prevent Wealth

In the end, no one gets married knowing that the relationship will end in a divorce, but as we all know, it sometimes happens. Before doing anything spiteful or more hurtful to our partner, it is best to communicate and express true feelings early so that if a divorce ultimately takes place, it can be on the most reasonable terms that will minimize how much wealth we prevent.

Our Marriages Often End in Divorce

Chapter 18

Our Social "Friends" and Other Distractions Limit our

Productivity

The concept of what a friend has become is so startling. Thanks to the Internet, and with exceptional thanks to Mark Zuckerberg's Facebook, the traditional definition of what we've had as a friend has been revolutionized.

My young son had confided in me about one such revolutionized relationship with a "friend" that had in my words, affected his life. He was playing a game on one of his video game consoles. In this game, one can make "friends" by interacting over an Internet-connected network with others as the game is being played. Eventually, with enough interactions with the same players, "friendships" are made.

It's really quite simple to make a "friend" with this game; it's as simple as three button presses on an interfacing controller. After the "friend" has been added to a friend's list, anytime the game console is turned on, the user will be alerted when a "friend" also turns on his game console if it is connected to the console's network. After several interactions over the Internet, these "friends" become supposedly "real friends." Without ever seeing this "friend," without ever having a conversation outside of an electronic chat, without ever sharing a brawl, without ever touching, a relationship is made.

My son had told me that his "friend" had made him upset one day, and that he was rather sad. His "friend" decided that he did not want to invite my son to play online that day, and his "friend" told him that he was too busy interacting with other online gamer "friends." Thus, my son became disappointed, and to my dismay, as a parent, I had to share that burden.

In my conversation with my son, I tried to explain to him what a true friend was: someone with whom you can sit down with, have a conversation with, play sports games with, and have a sleepover with. But am I wrong? Has the Internet really revolutionized what a friend has become?

As I pondered this question, I thought about the relationships that I had made over the Internet in my short time blogging and over few years that I had been taking online graduate courses. I too had never met the people with whom I've had online interactions with, but over several electronic conversations, connections were eventually made. More conversations had ensued, and I had begun to learn from my new "friends" and share past experiences—things that are fundamentally cherished in friendship. Although these shared experiences had been limited specifically to personal finance, they had been experiences nevertheless.

It has now become easier to find someone over the Internet who is interested in personal finance than it is to find someone with similar interests in person. Is it because it's just a fact, or is it because our lives have made it so? Unfortunately, I think that it's the former, especially when the majority of people's time is spent on the Internet. But then again, there is no coffee shop that advertises; *Only Personal Finance Discussions Here* any more than there is a school yard that advertises; *Only Little Big Planet Discussions Here.*

Around the same time that my son had confided in me, my spouse had did the same. She told me how she was kind of upset because her "friends" were going to sporting events that she had wished that she had the opportunity to attend. And she further told me how her friends were meeting the sports stars, which made her disappointments worse. And like my son, my spouse had never actually met these "friends," but their Internet relationship was built over time. Yet, she still was affected by the comments, pictures, and vacations of these "friends" because she had begun living vicariously through them. Is the new concept of "friend" just a temporary social phenomenon?

The time that is spent with our Internet "friends" is now limited only by time zones, so we can pretty much stay connected, especially with the tools that allow us to do so: laptops, smart phones, and tablets, among other things. Our friends in the past were limited by our routines. But now, our "friends" have become a part of our routines. Waking up in the morning, we can see what our "friends" did while we were asleep. While we are getting ready for work, we can see what our "friends" have posted on their blogs or "pages." While at work we can interact via our smart phones, and get the latest "statuses" or "tweets" of our friends. In between adding ingredients to our recipes while cooking dinner when we are finally home from work, we can still exchange a few chats. In between waking, going to work, cleaning, and up until we go to bed, we can and often do make our "friends'" lives our own. But in this new concept, does the new "friend" take away from family, or jobs, or our productivity? Are our "friends" just a convenient joy to past time? Are they better for us? Or do our connections become an addiction?

If it is true that time equals money, and money is earned by giving our time, does time excessively spent with our "friends" prevent us from earning money and therefore prevent our wealth? When it comes to a point where we can't even shut friends off and are expected to respond quickly to their "pokes," doesn't it take away from our productivity? Can't we do something else more meaningful? Have our "friends" really become so important that we allow those interactions to take away from who we are?

So like my son was affected by his "friend's" actions over his gaming network and like my spouse was affected by her vicarious desires, does your social "friends" affect your earning ability, productivity, or creativity? Are those relationships so important as to take away from our productivity?

How much of our time that we spend online can be spent instead on building a better relationship with our partners or children? How much of that time can be spent experiencing life? How much of that time could be spent by earning extra money, working on a novel, taking online classes, creating the next Facebook? How does your "friends" affect your earning ability? How does your "friends" affect your significant relationships? How do your friends prevent your wealth?

Our Social "Friends" and Other Distractions Limit our Productivity

Let me be clear, though, social networking, blogs, video games, books, and other things are not the enemy. We are in control. However, if we let these new social forms of engagement consume and affect our lives, we will no longer be in control. *We must all strive for the perfect work-life balance.* We must give ourselves a time limit on our engagements. We must figure out which ones are more important to our productivity and which of our "friends" are really helping us to grow. Because ultimately, taking in too much of one thing will always leave too little room for something else. *Always.* But I suppose what the question really boils down to is that of productivity, and do we understand the importance of a *work-life balance* concept?

The work-life balance concept is about prioritizing work and pleasures such as social networking, video games, and other things that may direct our attention away from securing our financial future. In order to maximize our financial future, we must never be complacent with our financial situation unless we have reached a point where we no longer are depending on others for our income; in many cases, few people have reached such a pinnacle. Therefore, we must balance pleasures with work. If we find that we are neglecting to do things such as continue our education or learn a new skill, or not doing things to maximize our earnings and therefore our marketability at work, then we must find an appropriate balance. Working on earning a degree as opposed to working to get to the next level in a video game will almost always be better for our financial future.

Some of us strive to achieve the work-life balance concept, yet we often fail, and it's acceptably understood given all of the distractions in the new world that we live in. We just have to keep striving to achieve balance. If we are not careful, we may find that our dealings with technology may cheat us out of *living*. Whether that living is through building a stronger relationship with the family, or giving more time to one's self by increasing one's education, whether formal or informal, we should try to lean towards these things prior to settling down into our virtual escapes.

Prior to playing a video game, writing a blog post, watching an hour of television, or whatever it is that we may struggle with, we must take a look around the house and ask ourselves, can our time be spent doing something better? Is the laundry put away or has it been in the dryer for several days now? Have I played the board game with my children that they received for Christmas or a birthday?

Have I read a book in a while that causes me to think and reflect? Is whatever it is that I am about to do going to help me or someone else grow?

If you are currently uncomfortable with your financial picture, you should ask yourself whether whatever it is that you long so much to do is going to help your financial future. Or will you continue your old ways, and thus prevent yourself from building wealth, even though wealth is knowingly within your reach?

Chapter 19

We Don't Have a Plan to Build Wealth

The unfortunate, but realistic truth in all of this is that many of us still will not understand the troubles that we put ourselves through until we wake up to find how low we have actually sunk. It won't be until we successfully prevent our wealth, that we realize the ramifications of our past actions. But by then, it may be too late. We may find ourselves working at age sixty, not because we want to, but because we have to. We will live vicariously through those who have actually made it, and envy their success.

We must resist the described extreme financial mistakes, and we must realize that we can live for today, but only if we are well prepared for tomorrow. Having learned throughout this book the ways that we prevent wealth, how should we actually build it? To put it simply, we have to be conscious to avoid doing the things that prevent our wealth. No one can guarantee riches in real estate. No one can guarantee success in the stock market. And no one can predict what tomorrow will bring. However, what we *can* predict is that if we heed the information presented in this book, wealth is within our reach, as long as we have given ourselves time to succeed.

We Don't Have a Plan to Build Wealth

Time is our true enemy, but it can also be on our side. The earlier we set a plan for wealth, the wealthier we can become. The earlier we realize our mistakes, the earlier we can turn them around.

Depending on how far we've sunk, wealth accumulation will not be easy, and for some it can be almost impossible. But what we can do is vow to live a better financial life composed of wiser financial decisions; decisions that does not burden us with debt payments, or led us to impulsive spending, but ones that well thought out and made consciously.

What is your vision? Think about it, and set goals to get there. Instead of simply living for today, plan for tomorrow. Does this mean that we can't buy the things that we want? Should we live a life of pure frugality? Should we not enjoy life's pleasures as they are presented? The short answer is no, as long as we have a strategic plan in place.

There are really only four main steps to build wealth. We must:

- **Define what wealth means to us.**
- **Determine what needs to happen to bring wealth within our reach.**

- **Set effective financial goals to meet our personal definition of wealth.**
- **Reevaluate our goals as necessary.**

I've learned that there is no magic formula for building wealth, although, a golden rule will sum it up: Make smart decisions! *After all, it's not how little we earn; it's the accumulation of unwise decisions that prevents us from building wealth.* For many, wealth accumulation is a slow process, but most of us can get there if we allow ourselves to do so. We must create a plan that we can commit to, but continually reevaluate it as necessary. Only then can we understand where we are going. Only then can we stop *preventing wealth.*

An Example of a Plan in Action:

Define what wealth means to me:

1) **Wealth is not working, unless I want to work.** If I enjoy what I do, then working won't be a problem, but if I don't enjoy what I do, I want to walk away, and not have to worry about how I'm going to pay my next month's bills. If I'm sleepy in the morning, I should be able to sleep

in. If I'm tired at work, I should be able to go home.

2) **Wealth should maximize my time.** If I want to take a month of travel, I should be able to do so, without answering to anyone, and not having anything to worry about. If I want to extend my vacation for a week or two, I should be able to do so. If my grandchildren have a school play, I should be able to attend, without any repercussions for taking off of work. After all, if I'm wealthy I wouldn't have to work.

3) **Wealth is helping others.** If there is someone in need, I should be able to give without hesitating to help. With minimum bills, and a steady stream of income, this would be no problem.

Determine what needs to happen to bring wealth within my reach:

1) If I pay off my home, my largest monthly expense should be gone in retirement.

2) If I start a plan now to ensure that my children's college tuition is covered before they actually

start college, I will not have that expense taking away from any retirement income.

3) If I save enough towards retirement such that I generate a healthy retirement income, I will not need to work.

4) If I appropriately insure myself, I can protect my assets, and subsequently my income generating ability.

Set effective financial goals to meet my personal definition of wealth:

1) I want my home to be paid off before I am forty-five years old. I am now thirty-years-old. In order to do this, I will mortgage my home for no more than 15 years. This means that I must refinance to correct my mistake of an original thirty year mortgage. This will not only pay off my home before I am 45, but it will minimize the interest that I pay, and help me actually build equity in the process. The $200,000 that I will save in interest by not using a thirty year mortgage, I can use to pay for other things. If I cannot refinance my home for whatever reason, I will affirm to make the extra monthly

payments so that my goal will still be met, while continually pursuing a refinance.

2) I will keep all of my debts minimized. I will try to pay cash for all things that I desire. I understand that the interest that I pay the banks is money that can go towards other goals.

3) I will build myself an emergency fund. This will cover unexpected expenses.

4) If I have to purchase a vehicle, I will purchase a reasonable car for a reasonable price that does not affect my effective financial goals. I understand that the more money that I spend on cars, the less money that I have to meet or apply towards other goals. If I have to finance a vehicle, it will never be for more than 36 months, and I will educate myself to understand the effect of high interest financing.

5) I will save at least $50,000 in college tuition for my child. If my child is now eight years old, I would have ten years to reach my goal. If I start this goal today, I will invest $416.66 monthly for college savings, nothing more and nothing less.

6)   I will save for an expected retirement income stream of $3500 monthly in an employee sponsored retirement plan, or in an IRA if time permits. This monthly stream will have to last me for thirty years. I will use a conservative estimate in a retirement income calculator (6% of growth) and save at least this monthly amount.

7)   I will purchase adequate insurance, so that my assets are protected. I will purchase full coverage for my vehicles, home insurance for my property, dental and medical insurance for my family, and disability insurance to protect my income. I will further purchase life insurance to protect my financial legacy, if I shall perish.

Reevaluate my goals as necessary:

I understand that my goals should be constantly evaluated to reflect my situation. I may decide that I'd rather purchase another home than the one I have. In any case, a paid off home should continue to be a retirement goal. Maybe the effect would be to push back my retirement

We Don't Have a Plan to Build Wealth

date. Either way, my plans may need to be adjusted to account for any life changes, seen or unseen.

Chapter 20

Conclusion: We Don't Understand That Time is Money

I hope that you've enjoyed reflecting with me. There are many other ways that we prevent wealth, but to expound on all of them will take plenty of your time. We can easily talk about how:

- We try to keep up with the Jones'
- We aren't very skeptical
- We buy things that we don't need
- We don't take advantage of offers
- We are too accustomed to hand-outs
- …And so on.
- …And so on.

But ultimately, we must also understand that time is money. And it is time that we can't get back. We can reflect forever, but I believe that you may now understand the underlying concepts in this personal reflection. I'd rather you spend your next hour or two reflecting on what you've learned. I thank you for reading this far, and I hope that you have enjoyed what you've read, but now the changes, if any are needed, are up to you.

If you have enjoyed what you read, please pass this book along to a friend. Hopefully a community of people will evolve that teaches others the mistakes that they have made. Hopefully we may learn from each other and ultimately make better financial decisions together. Remember, it's not how little we earn; it's the accumulation of unwise decisions that prevents us from building wealth.

How We Prevent Wealth

Endnotes

Chapter 2:

Danko, William D; Stanley, Thomas J. 1996. New York. *The Millionaire Next Door: The Secrets of America's Wealthy.*

Chapter 5:

[i] *Salary for All K-12 Teachers.* Retrieved from: http://www.payscale.com /research/US/All_k-12_Teachers/Salary

Chapter 13:

[ii] Ydstie, John. March 2010. 401(k)s *Still Fall Short as a Retirement Strategy.* http://www.npr.org/templates/story /story.php?storyId=124290221